S Stenhouse Publishers
Portland, Maine

Pembroke Publishers
Markham, Ontario

Teaching *with* Intention

Defining Beliefs, Aligning Practice, Taking Action

Debbie Miller

K–5

Stenhouse Publishers
www.stenhouse.com

Pembroke Publishers Limited
www.pembrokepublishers.com

Library of Congress Cataloging-in-Publication Data
Miller, Debbie, 1948–
    Teaching with intention : defining beliefs, aligning practice, taking action, K–5 / Debbie Miller.
        p. cm.
    Includes bibliographical references.
    ISBN 978-1-57110-387-1 (alk. paper)
    1. Elementary school teaching. 2. Effective teaching. I. Title.
    LB1555.M55 2008
    372.1102—dc22

                                                            2008016720

Cover, interior design, and typesetting by Martha Drury

Manufactured in the United States of America on acid-free, recycled paper
14 13 12 11 10 09   9 8 7 6 5 4

7/5/11

With love and admiration for Chad Miller, Katy Slocum, Kim Hulette, Courtney Miller, and thoughtful teachers like them who have the courage to think for themselves and the moxie to motivate their students to do the same

Contents

Acknowledgments

Some say we are judged by the company we keep. I hope that's true, because I'm delighted, honored, and grateful to keep company with so many wise, witty, and wonderful folks! Heartfelt thanks to . . .

My friends and colleagues at the Denver-based Public Education and Business Coalition and Regis University: You have influenced who I am as a teacher beyond measure. Thank you for inspiring me and so many others to do our best work in the classroom and beyond.

Maria Christina Williams: I'm so happy you took me by the hand that day and led me to your remarkable classroom. You were right when you said, "I think you'll like it here." Actually, dear heart, I loved it there!

Betsy Moreno: I'll never forget your kindness.

Katy Slocum, Valerie Burke, Val Livingston, Colleen Buddy, Shelley Schmitzer, Michelle DuMoulin, and Brenda Linder: The pleasure of working with you and your students (and in some cases taking pictures of your gorgeous classrooms) was all mine.

Dylan, Emelio, Charles, Roxie, Katie, Colin, and Torin: Teachers everywhere wish you were their students! I admire your spunk, your willingness to have a go at something new, and your permission for me to share your stories.

Beth Hudson and Phyllis Boller: I'm honored to have worked over time with you and the wonderful teachers and children in Junction City, Kansas. Long live the Shaved Ice Stand!

Philippa Stratton at Stenhouse: We did it again! Thank you for being such a thoughtful editor and great friend. Also kudos to Erin, Kate, Jay, and Nate and to all my buddies at Stenhouse—you really are the best.

Martha Drury: Your sense of design is, as always, magnificent! It's just the way I'd have done it, if only I knew how.

Ellin Keene: Hey, darlin'. You're my Number-One reader, writer, coffeemate, shopping-date friend! Thank you for years and years of conversation, collaboration, friendship, and fun. I thought this book might never see the light of day, but you always knew it would. Thank you for reading it "one more time" again and again and again.

Peter Johnston: Wow. I was sick in bed with day three of the flu when I received your response to *Teaching with Intention*. My husband read it aloud to me and an amazing thing happened. I jumped up and did a little dance! I wondered if this book would speak to you in some way, and I am incredibly honored that it did. Your work has meant so much to so many of us in the field.

Brenda Power, Franki Sibberson, Kristin Venable, Smokey Daniels, Pat Johnson, Kelley Dull, Barb Smith, William Hagood, and Sheila Swanson: Your careful reading and insightful responses always moved me forward. I'm forever grateful!

Joy Lowe: Is there a person on the planet with a more fitting first name? And do you ever want to hear, "Can you help me with these permissions?" again? (I didn't think so.) Thank you for all you do to keep me safe and sane when I'm on the road.

Noah, Chad, Courtney, and Rachel Miller: So now we have four! And maybe, one day, even more??? (No rush!) My heart is filled with love for you—thank you for being your sweet and loving selves, day in and day out.

And to Don: This really is the last one! Thank you for listening, being patient, and reading and responding in the kindest of ways. And so now, my love, are we ready to play? Grab the snorkels, pack the shorts, and let's sail away for a year and a day . . .

INTRODUCTION

Welcome, Reader!

■ ■ ■ ■ ■ ■

I still remember that hot day in June. There we were, my husband and I, packing up my classroom as I had done so many times before. But this time it wasn't just for the summer. This time it was for good.

Reading with Meaning had just come out, and the *Happy Reading!* videos were in the can. And I was leaving the classroom after teaching for thirty years in the Denver Public Schools. "Yikes!" I remember thinking. "What am I DOING? What was I thinking when I decided to launch a brand-new consulting career at this stage of my life?"

The teacher taking my place had chosen to move in on this very same day. Eager, sweet, and young, she asked if it would be better for her to wait; I said, "Don't be silly; it's fine." But inside I wondered for the umpteenth time if it was too late to change my mind.

And then out of the corner of my eye I noticed she put the meeting area in the entirely wrong place . . .

"You know," I wanted to say, "if you put it over in *this* corner, the sun slants in softly through the blinds in the early morning, setting the perfect tone for the read-aloud and lesson. And if you'd leave my desk how it was, *facing* the windows, you'd get to see the daffodils peeking their heads up through the snow in spring."

Reading my mind, my husband guided me out into the hall, gave me a hug, and said, "Debbie, stop. It's her turn now. And you always say that there's more than one way to do things, remember?"

I remembered.

We eyed the yellow cabinet with red trim standing tall in one corner, the only reminder of what was once the meeting area. "Are you sure you want to take it?" he asked. I knew it was heavy, I knew it meant another trip, and I knew by heart the names of those who wanted it. But I couldn't help myself. "I'm sure," I said.

And so, at the end of the day our basement was filled with the stuff of thirty years of teaching. Yellow cabinet included.

Over the summer I found myself going downstairs and just staring, for no particular reason. I had workshops, presentations, and demonstration lessons to prepare for, yet I couldn't seem to get a grip on how to put everything together. I began to wonder if I'd made the right decision; I began to wonder if I had anything to say to teachers at all.

Then I had a revelation! In the classroom I loved turning the lights down low at the end of the day, shutting the doors, savoring the calm and the quiet. I'd spread out the kids' work, their notebooks and mine, and take time to reflect on where we'd been, where we were now, and where it made the most sense to go next. I'd search for just the right books, plan whole- and small-group lessons, and think about how to move kids forward. I loved that time. And I really loved that place.

So what's a girl to do?

That very day I went back down into the basement, this time with a purpose and a plan. I unpacked most of the boxes we'd brought from school; partitioned off a little corner of the basement with bookshelves and organized the books; pushed and pulled the yellow cabinet with the red trim into the corner; lit the lamps; and, *voilà*! I had my place for planning and reflection back!

Okay. I know there were psychological issues going on here, but think *transition . . .*

And what did my husband have to say when I asked him if he thought this was all just a little too weird? "No," he mused, "it's not really all that weird. But if you start commandeering the kids from the neighborhood down here, I just might change my mind."

And so it makes sense that it was here, on the floor of my newly trans- ported meeting area, that I began to plan for my new life outside the classroom. It's been five years now, and while you might be relieved to know I've moved my work to the upper regions of our home, the meeting area is still intact, just in case the neighborhood kids *want* to come in and play a little school!

■■■

In these five years I've learned a lot. I've kept up with my reading, but it's conversations with teachers at seminars and conferences and working with children in classrooms across the country that have influenced my work most of all. And while I've said for years that there is more than one way to do things, I take an even longer, broader view now.

I'm convinced that success in the classroom depends less on *which* beliefs we hold and more on simply *having* a set of beliefs that guides us in our day-to-day work with children. Once we know who we are and what we're about in the classroom, we become intentional in our teaching; we do what we do *on purpose*, with good reason. Intentional teachers are thoughtful, reflective people who are conscious of the decisions they make and the actions they take; they live and teach by the principles and practices they value and believe in.

This is a book in two parts. In the first part, "Defining Beliefs and Aligning Practices," I share my beliefs about teaching and learning and encourage you (anew or for the first time) to think about and clearly define the principles and practices that guide you and your work with children.

The second part, "Taking Action," describes what it looks like for me when my beliefs and practices are aligned. Each chapter in this part begins with a belief statement and is followed by its application—what it looks like and how it sounds—in the classroom. The primary and intermediate classrooms I portray are real classrooms (with real kids!) that I've worked in since leaving my own.

When it comes to thinking about topics like defining beliefs, aligning practices, and taking deliberate action to set things in motion, you might be wondering, "Debbie. Who has the time? What's the point?" The point is this: We're professionals; we need to make full use of our professional autonomy.

Most chapters have a small section called Something to Try. These are optional opportunities (of course!) for you to think about what you believe about teaching and learning. I know it's challenging to find time in the day for reflection—it may feel like just one more thing to add to the list that never seems to end. And yet if we don't, where does that leave us? If we aren't thoughtful, reflective, and strategic teachers, can we expect our children to be thoughtful, reflective, and strategic readers, writers, and thinkers?

In these times of scripted programs and prepackaged materials I know it may be tempting to surrender. But who among us is going to keep up the good fight? Who among us is willing to stand up for what we know is right? I'm in, and I hope you are, too. Happy Reading!

PART I

Defining Beliefs *and* Aligning Practices

CHAPTER 1

Picture Perfect:
How Does Your Ideal
Classroom Look,
Sound, *and* Feel?

■ ■ ■ ■ ■ ■ ■

If I were to ask you to close your eyes and envision the perfect classroom scene, what would you see? What would you hear and smell and feel? Think big! If everything were going just the way you'd like it to, what would be happening? What would your kids be doing? How about you?

Maybe you've observed such a classroom or maybe it's one you've always pictured in your mind's eye. Either way, once you take the time to envision exactly what it is you want for you and the children you teach, you can set about taking action and bringing your vision to life. And if you were to ask me the same questions, how would I answer?

I'd begin by telling you about a real third-grade classroom I visited recently in a little school just outside Cincinnati, Ohio. I arrive a little over an hour early (who knew I wouldn't get lost?) and decide to walk around a bit, just to get a feel for the school where I'll be working for the next few days. So I'm walking down the hall, admiring children's artwork that decorates the walls, when a little girl with a bright yellow office pass in hand comes up to me and says, "Are you the one who wrote that book? You should come see my room!" I learn that her name is Maria Christina Williams—"The Maria Christina is from my grandmother and the Williams from my dad"—and in no time she's got her hand in mine. She leads me to room 27, pulls out a chair, and says, "I think you'll like it here."

Like it here? That would be an understatement. I loved it there! I loved it there so much that it was really hard to leave. Sometimes teachers ask me if I miss the classroom. I don't miss it every day (thirty years is a long time!) but on that day, oh, my goodness, on that day, every part of me ached to be back.

What made it so hard to leave? So many things! And with the help of my notes and a few photographs I took while I was there, I'll put myself back inside teacher Betsy Moreno's classroom and relive (with pleasure!) what it was like on the day I was so kindly escorted into her room.

■ ■ ■

I see kids gathered around tables, desks, and rugs on the floor, reading and interacting in a variety of authentic ways to picture books, poetry, chapter books, magazines, nonfiction, and more. They're working independently, with partners, and in small groups. I hear the buzz of conversation and collaboration. Almost everywhere I look I see evidence of rigorous, joyful learning.

The room's organized. From books to materials, it's clear there's nothing random here. Books are mostly in tubs and baskets throughout the room, labeled for easy access by series, author, topic, type of text, or level (see Figure 1.1 in the color insert). A collection of anthologies lines one shelf. I watch two children talking quietly in the meeting area, browsing through a basket of books. Before I know it, they find just the book they're looking for.

Paper, markers, scissors, and more are organized on a shelf, accessible to all. Two children carefully tape the torn page of a well-loved book, another matter-of-factly fills the stapler. I wince when its long arm springs forward, but there's no need for worry. This child knows exactly what he's doing.

The walls of the classroom speak; student work and anchor charts are everywhere (see Figure 1.2 in the color insert). New learning and the mental processes readers, writers, mathematicians, and scientists use to construct meaning and enhance comprehension are made visible, public, and permanent. The questions, ideas, and big understandings recorded sound like real voices of real kids. "Come learn with us!" they seem to say.

I see a huge chart along one wall that showcases student learning and thinking about the Underground Railroad, detailing not only the learning but its source, relevant vocabulary, student questions about this time and place in history, and children's handwritten responses (see Figure 1.3 in the color insert). I can tell they've been reading historical fiction up to now—books including *Barefoot, Escape on the Underground Railroad, Sweet Clara and the Freedom Quilt, Follow the Drinking Gourd, Freedom River*, and *Journey to Freedom: A Story of the Underground Railroad* line the ledge below the chart. I can't help but think that once kids get into that tall stack of textbooks nearby, they'll have so much background knowledge that understanding the content will be a breeze!

Three boys off in a distant corner attract my attention. They're crowded around a copy of Tony Johnston's *The Harmonica* (2004), talking and writing, mostly about their impressions of the story, but also last night's soccer game. They can't believe they beat The Crush! I smile at the soccer talk—if you beat The Crush, wouldn't you just have to talk about it, too?

The Harmonica—a powerful picture book inspired by the life of a young Holocaust survivor—is a story about a family split apart when Nazi soldiers invade Poland. When the commandant of the camp forces the little boy to play the harmonica for him night after night, the boy thinks of "my

FIGURE 1.4
"Whoa. That's a good one!" One
child's synthesis of *The
Harmonica* by Tony Johnston.

FIGURE 1.4
"Whoa. That's a good one!" One child's synthesis of *The Harmonica* by Tony Johnston.

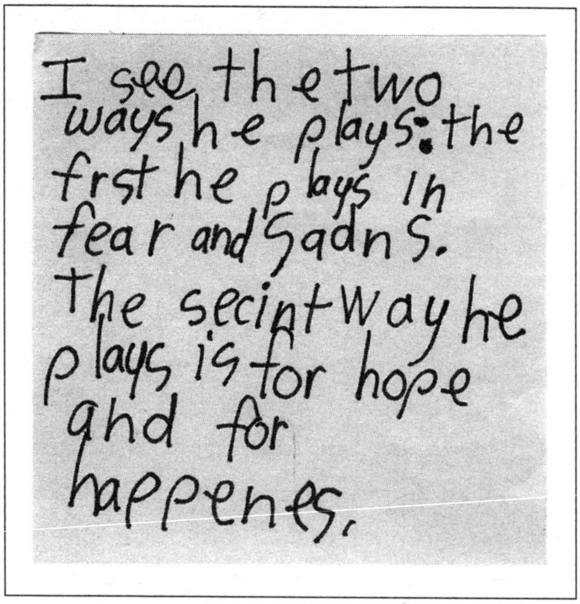

father, who had given it to me. Of my mother, who once had danced. And of prisoners, without hope, who might hear the notes and be lifted, like flight of birds."

"Let's go back to this page," says one boy who wears a grass-stained black-and-white soccer shirt, "this one here, where he goes back to the camp and someone whispers, 'Bless you' in his ear. Look what I wrote."

And he proceeds to read these words from a small blue sticky note (Figure 1.4): "I see the two ways he plays. The first he plays is in fear and sadness. The second way he plays is for hope and happiness."

"Whoa," says another boy in the group. "That's a good one. I never thought about it like that before."

"Me neither," says the third. "That is reallyreallyreally good. You should go and stick that on the Synthesizing *The Harmonica* chart" (see pp. 61–62).

I'm in love. I think it's reallyreallyreally*really* good. And I've never thought about it like that before either.

And it's apparent that the Harmonica Kids are not the only ones having conversations that focus on big ideas . . .

"Do you get this part? Why would some of the black people NOT want to escape to freedom on the Underground Railroad?"

"When the shoes say, 'Step inside, we're big and bruised and scuffed, but down past the tough we've worn ourselves soft,' do you think it's about the grandpa, too? Like the shoes and grandpa are both deep down warm and fuzzy inside?"

"Let's go get the Leo Lionni tub! He's my favorite author and I want to study all his books. Let's make a list and then we can check them off after we read them!"

"Hey! Where's the teacher?" I suddenly wonder. It dawns on me that in the midst of falling in love, curious kids, and walls that talk, I'm not even sure she's in the room. And then I spot her, seated next to a child, eye-to-eye, conferring. This lucky boy has his teacher's full attention. No one is looking at the clock; there's not a hint of rush. There's simply the luscious feeling of endless time.

Next, she quietly gathers up a small group of children for a quick lesson on book selection . . .

"Girls and boys," she begins, "I was looking through your conferring notebooks—these right here—last night after school, and guess what I learned about you as readers? What do you think all of you have in common?"

She acknowledges their responses as thoughtful ones, and says, "When I conferred with each of you last week about the books you were reading, I noticed that N'Dia's books were all fiction, Jade's and James's books were all nonfiction, and Bianca's books were all poetry! And as I look back through your conferring notebooks, it's been that way for a while. Think about that a minute. What else do you know about yourselves and each other as readers?"

Students and their teacher have a conversation about what else they know, and before she leaves them, she says, "So . . . are you up for a challenge? Perfect! Let's try this. For the rest of this week, finish up with the books you have. On Friday afternoon, when everyone chooses their books for next week, I want you to be adventurous! When you choose your new books, make sure that you have some fiction, nonfiction, and poetry in your selections. Take your time, and make thoughtful choices.

"It might be a good idea to talk with each other—I bet Bianca has some great poetry suggestions, James and Jade know a lot about nonfiction, and we know that N'Dia knows fiction. Right? So I'm asking you to think about what you know about yourselves as readers, the suggestions of your friends, and what you know about the other books in our library to make good choices. Does that make sense?

"Great! Why don't you talk a little bit about that now? I can't wait to see what you choose, and what you learn about yourselves and each other as readers next week!" And it's here that she leaves them.

The soulful voice of Keb Mo singing "I'm Amazing" is all it takes for these kids and their teacher to gather in the meeting area.

The Harmonica Kids open the discussion by sharing their thinking about the differences between retelling and synthesizing. Their theory is that if everyone were to retell *The Harmonica*, the retellings would be very much the same. But if everyone were to synthesize it, the syntheses would sound "totally different." And then they want to know what everyone else thinks about that. Kids seem to know just how to join into the discussion. They talk and look at *each other*; responses are not directed to the teacher unless she joins in with a question or comment. And no one feels the need to raise their hand.

And what's the teacher doing during all of this? She's off to the side, listening carefully, taking notes. The kids are very much in charge.

I find myself thinking about that room, those kids, and their teacher well into the night. Could it have all come together due to some magical alignment of the stars? Could it be that this teacher, by some lovely quirk of fate, got all the brilliant, motivated, well-behaved children? Deep down I think we both know the answer. *Not a chance*. Deep down, I'm pretty certain her classroom looks and feels this way every year.

CHAPTER 2

Defining Beliefs *and* Aligning Practices

■ ■ ■ ■ ■ ■ ■ **M**y visit to Maria Christina's classroom—let's call it our anchor classroom from now on—was in early April, but back in September, way before leaves began to fall or rain gave way to snow, I'm betting that classroom didn't look at all the way it does now. I'm betting those kids didn't sound or act the way they did the day I stepped inside. And I'm betting their teacher, Mrs. Moreno, didn't either.

But the odds are good that she had a vision then of what she wanted for her kids in the weeks and months ahead, *and that she's made conscious decisions and taken deliberate actions to get them there ever since.* When teachers have a set of beliefs that guides our work, we know where we're going. There may be twists and turns along the way, but we always know where we're headed. When we know what we want for our kids in March, April, and May, we can set about getting them there starting in September.

When colleagues and I were studying with Brian Cambourne at Regis University in Denver, part of our coursework was to make explicit our beliefs about teaching and learning. We came together before, during, and after class to read and examine books, articles, and what seemed like reams of research; we tried things out with the kids in our classrooms; we reflected and wrote about what we were learning in our notebooks; and we engaged in conversations with colleagues about our reflections, teaching experiences, and current practices.

As Shelley Harwayne writes,

> *Classroom practice must be based on richly understood and deeply held beliefs about how children learn to read. In other words, what teachers say and do and how they engage children in reading acts must have theoretical underpinnings. Their practice is not based on a publisher's set of teacher directions or a handbook filled with teaching tips, but on concepts they themselves have examined carefully.*
> (2000, 207)

Through this process, each of us developed individual belief statements that synthesized our understanding of the research, the theories and classroom practices of others, and the collective knowledge of our years in the classroom.

This will probably come as no surprise, but the beliefs that guide me in my teaching are similar to the beliefs that guide Betsy Moreno. These are my beliefs:

- Classroom environments are most effective when they are literate and purposeful, organized and accessible, and, most of all, authentic.
- We cannot underestimate the power of our influence—what we choose to say and do in the classroom profoundly affects the ways children view their teacher, themselves, and each other.
- Learning is maximized when the lessons I design are purposeful, interactive and engaging, with real world applications.
- The gradual release of responsibility instructional model, integrated into a workshop format, best guides children toward understanding and independence (Pearson and Gallagher 1983).
- Formative, ongoing assessment enlightens and informs my day-to-day work with children.
- A workshop format based on the elements of time, choice, response, and community fosters active, responsive teaching and learning (Hansen 1987).

Defining my beliefs about teaching and learning took the better part of a year. It was the first time I'd thought about developing my own philosophy of teaching and learning—I'd always figured that was something somebody else did for me.

There are lots of "somebody elses" who would certainly like to! They'll even package it up pretty and tell us just what to say. But for all their pomp, it's hard to imagine the circumstance where prepackaged programs and scripts teach children better than we do. *We're* the ones in the unique and wonderful position to know where our kids have been, where they are now, and where it makes the most sense to take them next. *Real life isn't scripted. Neither is real teaching.*

Matching Beliefs and Practices

Once I developed my belief statements, the next step was to align them with my classroom practices. I looked closely at everything I did; I looked closely at everything I asked kids to do. From the beginning strains of the song "Oh What a Beautiful Morning" at the start of the day through the final chorus of "Happy Trails to You" at day's end, everything came under scrutiny. Nothing was sacred.

I'd ask myself questions about my practice: Where's the evidence of this belief in the classroom? What kinds of things should I be seeing, hearing, doing to support this belief? Where does this practice fit into what I say I value? What studies support this practice?

Whenever I found instances when my beliefs and practices were at odds (and there were more than you might think!), I had to make tough decisions. Would I change the statement *or* the practice? More often than not, it was the practice that was out of sync. I discovered that even though I'd *say* I believed in something, I'd find myself doing things, and asking kids to do things, that had me scratching my head.

Like the time I was thinking aloud as I read *The Midas Touch* to a group of first graders. We'd been working on ways to figure out the big ideas in our reading, and I was certain they'd "get" at least one of the big ideas—that being greedy or wanting too much can get us into big trouble. But no. They had other ideas. From their responses, it seemed as if they'd heard an entirely different story than the one I'd just read. The more they talked, the more I tried to set them straight. "Yeah, but . . . , Yeah, but . . . , Yeah, but . . . ," I'd say, over and over again.

Finally, Rachel ended the misery by standing up and practically yelling, "Okay, everybody. DON'T YOU GET IT? The theme is, Don't be greedy because it can get you into big trouble."

In the ensuing silence Rachel's words echoed in my head. In that moment I realized that I was the one not getting it. So intently was I listening *for* thinking that mirrored my own that I'd forgotten the importance of listening *to* what kids have to say. I barely heard them because I was so determined to lead them to my way of thinking.

I believe in the power of collaborative classroom communities where everyone's ideas are valued and respected. But had you been in my classroom that day, you'd never have known it. You'd have thought I believed that I was the one with all the answers.

It was this heightened sense of awareness that helped me determine whether my classroom practices and belief statements were a match. Had I not done my homework (and schoolwork, too!), I might never have thought much about the why and the how of my teaching. It would more than likely have been a little bit of this and a little bit of that. It was the process of defining and aligning that made all the difference.

It wasn't a walk in the park. I struggled. Sometimes it felt like I was trying to traverse the Rocky Mountains (and I don't even ski). And yet now, looking back, I see that it was the single most significant action I've taken as a teacher. It was precisely *because* of the struggle that I was able—in the end—to clearly articulate my beliefs about teaching and learning, cite the supporting research, and speak to its application in the classroom. Had it been easy, or had I let someone else do the thinking for me, my years in the classroom would not have been nearly so sweet.

My Wish for You

I wish the same for you. If you haven't already, this is the perfect time to do some thinking about what you believe about teaching and learning. Whether you're a beginning teacher or a veteran, the time is right to trust yourself and begin the process of defining your beliefs and aligning your practices.

You might begin, just like I did, by getting together with a small group of colleagues to talk about your current thinking about teaching and learning. Think about things like these:

- How do you go about teaching kids something new?
- What principles guide you?
- How do you know if kids are getting it?
- What do you do when they don't?

You might also want to read books and articles together and have conversations about what you read, share classroom experiences and current practices, and try out new things. Observe one another teaching. Question each other and yourselves. Take your time. No rushing allowed!

Through it all, consider keeping a notebook. I once heard Donald Graves say that writing is the ultimate form of synthesis. It's true! Record your observations, reflections, new thinking, learning, and questions. Ask yourself, "What do I value?"

When I think back to my days at Regis, it seemed like we were always being asked, "So, what are you thinking? Take a few minutes to reflect in your notebooks."

At first it felt weird. But when I'd look up and see that everybody else was writing, I'd say to myself, "Okay, Debbie. You're just going to sit there and *pretend*? Stop doodling and see what you can learn."

I learned plenty. Most of all, I learned the importance of slowing down and being present, of taking the time to think about and develop ideas, synthesize new learning, and write about what I had learned about my kids or myself as a teacher that day. And what that might mean for the days ahead.

Try it! Take fifteen minutes or so at the end of the day to reflect on what you've learned. Write it down. Write it any old way; it's only for you. After you've done this consistently—say, three or so times a week for a month or two—go back through your entries, see what you notice, and begin writing your belief statements. If you're like me, you'll revise, rewrite, scratch out, and start over, but it's important to begin. Keep your statements short, clear, potent, and powerful. Memorize them; put them up somewhere where you can see them every day. Let them guide your work.

What if you have district mandates that run counter to your beliefs? Take the high road. Don't let them defeat you. Do what you have to do; in the end no one can mandate how you feel about children, the ways you interact with them throughout the day, and the things you say and do that reflect who you are and what you believe about teaching and learning.

PART II

Taking Action

CHAPTER 3

Environment, Environment, Environment

I believe that classroom environments are most effective when they are literate and purposeful, organized and accessible, and, most of all, authentic.

■ ■ ■ ■ ■ ■ ■

I'm headed up the stairs and down the hall to Katy Slocum's fifth-grade classroom in Denver. It's lunchtime and it's all I can do to make my way through the throngs of kids hopping, skipping, and yakkity-yakking their way to the lunchroom.

I haven't met Katy yet, but a mutual friend has hooked us up. She knew I was interested in trying out some new ideas with kids around book selection, and Katy, a first-year teacher, had been thinking about that, too. We are all set to meet in her classroom over lunch and plan together for the days ahead.

We munch our way through Subway sandwiches, two teachers talking school. I listen to Katy describe her first few months of teaching, and it's not long before I realize that lessons on book selection are going to have to wait a while. Right now there are more important things on Katy's mind.

In September Katy had a pretty clear picture in her head of how she wanted things to be. Now it's November and that vision seems just a little hazy. She has that What did I get myself into? look.

"So, what things are bugging you most?" I ask her. "What's preventing you from teaching the way you believe is best for kids?"

Katy lets loose.

"I haven't really been able to do the kinds of things I learned about in school," she says. "There's so much other stuff I have to do that I never have time to do the things I really want to do. It's like there are two voices inside my head; one voice says, 'Do this, Katy, do that, Katy,' and the other one says, 'Slow down, Katy! Do what you know is right.' The do-this-Katy, do-that-Katy voice seems to be winning all the time now.

"And then there's the meeting area—it's too small and all twenty-five of us can't fit without sitting on top of each other, so we don't really go there much anymore. Now I stand up front, teaching kids at their seats, and it doesn't feel right. It seems so much about me, and not enough about them. I didn't even want there to *be* a front of the room, but now here I am, day after day, lecturing away.

"I want kids to choose the books they read, but right now they really can't. I have boxes of books—some I haven't even opened yet, but I haven't had time [Katy was hired two days before school began] to even see what I have or organize them. I'm not even sure where to begin and how to go about it. And some of them are so old—have you ever heard of *The Five Little Peppers and How They Grew*? [Actually, yes!]

"And everything feels so junky. I can't find things. Kids can't find things. It feels like stuff is everywhere—just look at my desk and their cubbies!"

She's not exaggerating. The cubbies—black plastic magazine holders—are jammed every which way with papers, pencils, note cards, books, math worksheets, rulers, homework, markers, and un-spiraling spiral notebooks.

And the stuff? It *is* everywhere (see Figure 3.1a, b, and c). Piles of paper lie on every conceivable surface, vying for space with stacks of books and magazines, cans full of scissors, paper clips and staple removers, CSAP (Colorado Student Assessment Profile) Practice Books, backpacks, plastic bags from Safeway filled with ingredients for science experiments, and an assortment of huge three-ring binders containing a variety of curriculum guides, some dating as far back as 1994.

Large brown grocery boxes advertising the likes of Downy Fabric Softener, Scott Paper Towels, and New Improved Tide are stacked high on the uppermost shelves, sporting different labels now: Bronco Math. Fabric. Butterfly Nets. Shakespeare Costumes. Plaster of Paris. Test Tubes. Old Science Textbooks.

"I have no idea who left them, or why," she tells me. "And I can't just throw them away." It's all I can do to stop myself from blurting, "Oh-yes-you-can-let's-do-it-right-now," but at the moment, I'm all about listening.

She wants the anchor charts she's made with the kids visible, but the fire marshal has been in, and there are restrictions about what and how much can go up on the walls. So, carefully made charts are here and there, rolled up and not, wrinkled, tearing, and looking less and less important.

And Katy wants to love the space where she and her kids work every day. She wants it to feel cozy. She hates the overhead lights. She wants lamps. A rug. And a pretty tablecloth.

I can tell she's not nearly finished, but we're interrupted by cries of, "Miss Slocum! Miss Slocum! Where have you *been*?"

"It's *freezing* out there!"

"We've been waiting for you to pick us up *forever*!"

"I just wish I could start over," Katy whispers.

"You know," I say, "we could do that."

And we—Katy, the kids, and I—do.

Katy may only be in her first few months of teaching, but already she understands the difficulty of trying to teach in an environment that doesn't support what she believes about teaching and learning. She's

FIGURE 3.1A
Katy's wondering, "Now, where *is* my notebook?"

FIGURE 3.1B
Katy's kids are wondering the same thing!

FIGURE 3.1C
When Katy and I found this portable blood pressure machine behind closed cupboard doors, I thought, "I think I might need this right about now!"

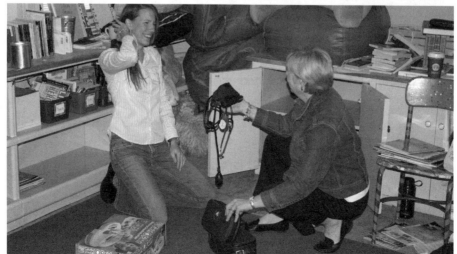

unable to put into place what she believes is best for kids because the environment will not allow it. The environment has hijacked everything she holds dear.

And not only is teaching difficult in such an environment, but learning is challenging, too. When things are going awry for teachers, things are probably not going so well for kids either.

Katy was serious when she whispered, "I just wish I could start over." And so was I when I whispered back, "We could do that." We agreed that getting the room in order was our first priority, and following that, we'd set about implementing routines, rituals, and predictable structures that kids and Katy could count on day after day.

We also wanted to bring Katy's kids into the mix. Publicly acknowledging pressing issues and asking kids what they think sends the message, "We're in this together. I'm listening and I care about you and what you're thinking. Let's figure out what we can do to make things better."

When Katy asked her kids what was bugging *them* most, when she asked what was preventing them from learning the kinds of things she was working so hard to teach them, they spoke right up.

- There's not enough room to spread out/we don't even have room to walk.
- I can never find my stuff/the cubbies aren't working.
- We don't like assigned seats/we want to choose where we sit.
- I don't like how the books are arranged/I can't find the ones I want.
- We hardly get to read/we really want to!
- We need more books/where's the nonfiction?
- I want it to be clean and cozy/it's hard to work when it's messy.
- I like when we meet together, but it's way too crowded/we can't even think and we get way too rowdy.

First Things First—Clear the Decks!

Before we can begin to rearrange furniture, organize books and materials, create literate environments, or even think about lamps, rugs, and pretty tablecloths, we've got to get rid of the things we don't need so we can make room for the things that we do. For Katy and I, that means making three piles:

1. things to keep
2. things someone else might want—maybe other teachers, kids, or Goodwill
3. things to throw away

We begin early one morning, tossing or organizing all those piles of paper, figuring out what to do with that tall tilting stack of *National Geographic* magazines and those cardboard boxes labeled so carefully by teachers who have come before. When the kids arrive, we scrunch ourselves into the meeting area, share our thinking, invite input, and ask for volunteers to help organize and put together all the books and materials for writing, science, social studies, and math. The rest agree to tackle their cubbies, desks, backpacks, and the floor.

Once the major surfaces are cleared—or at least ordered in some way—we move on, working after school to sort through closets, drawers, and all that was behind those closed cupboard doors.

We send three bright yellow Judy Clocks, two boxes of teddy-bear counters, and an extra box of 500 Unifix cubes to kindergarten and first grade. The bulk of the magnifying glasses, microscopes, magnets, test tubes, and potting soil go to the science lab. Twenty-five boxes of paper clips (what's that about?) go back to the office, along with bags of rubber bands, brads, thumbtacks, and six one-gallon jars of paste.

An amazing assortment of clothing items left behind by teachers goes into the Goodwill pile—cardigan sweaters, see-through plastic raincoats, scarves, umbrellas, shoes, and one never-worn pair of sequined St. Paddy's Day socks.

Outdated maps and globes go into the never-see-the-light-of-day pile. Ditto the ancient jigsaw puzzles of cats and puppies, the six dried-out Twirl-a-Paint kits, and the once-white Lite-Brites, minus their pegs. We toss out what seem like hundreds of old workbooks in every subject imaginable, reams and reams of yellowed and brittle handwriting paper, shoe boxes overflowing with broken crayons, used-up pencils and congealed bottles of glue, fuzzy-tipped markers, and twenty almost-empty tubes of glitter. Not to mention the packs and packs of faded construction paper and box after box of empty (and thankfully clean) baby-food jars.

And the two huge gray filing cabinets, filled to the top with teaching units, worksheets, lesson plans, and month-by-month themes and activities? I leave their fate and what's inside to Katy, but encourage her to be ruthless, and to consider getting rid of at least one of those metal giants entirely.

With all that stuff out of the way, no one could believe how much larger the classroom had become! And now, Katy could do some real thinking about her beliefs, the physical space and room arrangement, organizing all those books and materials, and creating a working, literate environment.

And, as you just might know, clearing the decks isn't always about getting rid of someone *else's* stuff. I was excellent at squirreling away all kinds of things, in all kinds of places, entirely on my own! Think bags (and bags) of pinecones for Thanksgiving turkey-making (it looked like fun in *Family Circle* a few years ago), stacks of find-a-word puzzles and coloring sheets (dropped off by a well-meaning parent), and that red folder filled with important papers I've stashed away (somewhere) for safekeeping.

I'd pledge to clean and organize a drawer or shelf a day on many a Monday morning, but I could never seem to keep that going much beyond Wednesday. My best strategy was to come to school on an occasional Saturday morning armed with a box of trash bags, a full-to-the-top bottle of Formula 409, a brand-new roll of paper towels, a sugar-free vanilla latte, and a Van Morrison CD. Cleaning, sipping, and singing "On the Bright Side of the Road" with Van—does it get any better than this?

We'd better hope so! But when I walk outside two or three hours later with a smile on my lips and a skip in my step, I'm not so sure.

And now I'm thinking the smile and the skip were about more than having a clean and uncluttered classroom. Could it be that clearing the physical clutter of my room also cleared the mental clutter in my mind?

☑ Something to Try

Step outside your classroom door and look back in, as if for the first time. What do you see? Do you want to go back inside? Or do you want to run and hide? If you're inclined to run, force yourself back. Grab your notebook and divide a page into thirds. In the first column, draw or write about what you like about your classroom environment. What seems to be working?

In the next column, do the same with what bothers you most. What's getting in the way of teaching and learning? What doesn't make sense? And in the last column, write or draw what you'd *like* to see when you step inside. Do the same from a child's point of view. Get at their eye level and see things as they see them. *Now* what do you see?

First impressions count. Classroom environments vary, but they always need to be *welcoming* places; interesting, joyful places that beckon kids and teachers to actively participate in the pursuit of knowledge. Places that invite curiosity, exploration, collaboration, and conversation. Places that make us want to come in and stay, day after day after day.

Next, consider asking a colleague—someone you trust in the field, but probably not a close friend—to step inside your room. Ask this person to take a few minutes to look around and then ask them the following kinds of questions:

- What do you know I value?
- What do you know about what I believe about teaching and learning? What's the evidence?
- What do you know about the kids in this room?

Any thoughtful person who spends even a small amount of time in our classrooms should be able to respond to these questions. If they can't, or if they say something that seems to us totally off the mark, it should give us pause. We have to wonder what it is about the environment that's sending mixed signals or no signals at all. Just as it's important to define our beliefs and align our practices, it's important to create classroom environments that reflect our beliefs.

Creating Your Thinking Classroom

Let's say school starts in a few weeks, or maybe, like Katy, you've been in school a while. Maybe it's even January! No matter when it is, once you've dealt with the stuff you don't need to make room for the things that you do, it's the perfect time to make certain that your environment supports what you believe about teaching and learning.

One way to begin is to ask yourself questions like these:

- Will children and I need a meeting area? Why? How will I/we use it? Can it be used for more than one purpose? Where will it go?
- Do children and I need areas for pairs and small groups of kids to work together? How will they be used? How many will we need? How will I define these spaces?
- What about kids' desks or tables? How will they be configured? Why this way?
- Where will kids keep their books, notebooks, pencils, paper, backpacks, etc.?
- Do I want writing, math, science, and social studies areas? Why? What will be their purpose—will kids come here to work, or is the space for organization and accessibility of materials? Where will these areas be in the room?
- What about books? Do I want them in one area, or throughout the room? Why? Who will organize them, and how?
- Computers? How many do I have? How many do I need? Do they all work? How will they be used?
- What about my desk? Do I need it? How will I use it? Where will it go?

There are no wrong answers. What matters most is that you take some time to be thoughtful about questions like these and decide for yourself what will make the most sense for you and the students you teach. The decisions you make will reflect what *you* believe about teaching and learning.

Here is how I answered several of these questions while planning at the start of the year, and how my answers affected my classroom design.

Do children and I need a meeting area?

Yes. A meeting area is the one place in the room we can all come together, and children and I use it in a variety of purposeful ways throughout the day, including opportunities for the following:

- explicit teaching, modeling, and teacher/student demonstrations, often within the context of shared reading, read-alouds, think-alouds, and interactive read-alouds;
- classroom discussions, turning and talking in twos and threes, getting eye-to-eye and knee-to-knee for focused discussion;
- kids and teachers to reflect, share, and teach each other what they've learned about themselves as readers, writers, mathematicians, and scientists that day; and
- partner and small-group work, conferring, and independent practice, when we're not using it in the ways I just described.

To accommodate this kind of work, the meeting area needs to be large enough so that everyone can fit inside comfortably. Mine is in a corner of the room, defined by two walls, low sets of bookshelves, tubs of books labeled in a variety of ways for easy access, a chair, a rug, a lamp, and a yellow cabinet with red trim. A bulletin board for anchor charts and student work lines one wall, and books and a whiteboard (for the morning message and announcements) are propped onto the chalkboard ledge.

Sometimes we think about meeting areas as something for primary classrooms only. I disagree. There's something powerful about bringing kids together, often with clipboards and pencils in hand, and asking them to listen to or read a short, thought-provoking piece of text, write a response, and turn and talk with each other about both the content and the processes they used to make meaning. It forces the matter—this is what we're about, this is how it sounds, this is how we learn.

A small basket filled with things I/we might need is on the floor by my chair—things like dry erase and permanent markers, Sharpies, vis-a-vis pens, sticky notes in different sizes, scissors, tape, a stapler, a small bottle of glue, and a class set of sharpened pencils. Clipboards and small dry erase boards are kept in a small crate in this area, too—everything we might need at any time close by.

There's an intimacy in coming together, asking questions, thinking about big ideas, and synthesizing new learning that's less likely to happen when kids are at their seats. Whether the focus is reading, math, writing, social studies, or science, a meeting area can be the perfect place for modeling, thinking aloud, discussion, and demonstration, no matter what the subject or grade. I guarantee it—you create it, they will come!

Do children and I need areas for small-group work?

Yes. Just like the meeting area, small-group spaces are used in a variety of purposeful ways throughout the day:

- when the whole class is working in small groups in response to a particular text, topic, theme, or problem;
- for teacher-guided, needs-based groups;
- for book clubs or literature circles, both formal and spontaneous;
- when kids decide to work together for a specific purpose;
- for partner reading/partner work; and
- as quiet workplaces for those who need them.

Because I use the gradual release of responsibility instructional model (Pearson and Gallagher 1983), with its phases of teacher modeling and guided and independent practice, these kinds of areas are essential. The meeting area is perfect for whole-group teaching, thinking aloud, and modeling, but when children are ready to assume more responsibility for their learning—but not yet ready to apply the skill or strategy independently—working together in pairs or small groups is just the kind of support they need.

And working independently doesn't always mean working in isolation. Having areas where children can get together to discuss big ideas, solve problems, research a topic of mutual interest, or learn to read and talk about a book together can enhance their understanding and help them construct meaning through conversation and collaboration.

Depending on the number of children I have that year, I usually set up about five areas for small-group work. The meeting space can easily be used for two areas, with three or more additional areas throughout the room. I define the places with bookshelves, a rug, or a small table and chairs. Want tables but you've no room for chairs? Take the extenders off your table legs and kids can sit on carpet squares or pillows on the floor.

Do children and I need a library area?

No need for a library area; I want the *whole room* to feel like a library! I love having books everywhere, organized in a variety of ways for easy access throughout the day, every day. When children are *surrounded* by books, we're showing them that reading is important throughout the day; reading is infused into almost everything we do. It's as if the books are inviting us in. "Take a look at me!" they seem to say. "I'm really good inside."

If tubs of books are placed throughout the room rather than in just one area, it eliminates the mob scenes that result when twenty-seven children fall all over themselves and each other trying to get at the books they want. It's difficult to select books with purpose and intention in situations like these; wouldn't you take almost any book you could get your hands on, just to avoid the crush?

Books are organized in small plastic tubs, and I am careful not to stuff them so full that books are difficult to pry out, or too heavy for children to carry. Two tubs of books containing fifteen titles each is better than one tub jammed with thirty.

Book tubs are labeled in a variety of ways, most often by author, series, genre, topic, and level. Again, there is no right or wrong way to organize books in your classroom library. What's important is to take a good look at what you have, and think about what will make the most sense for you and your kids. Involving kids in figuring out how to categorize and label books is one of the many ways we can make our thinking visible and begin to build trust and independence early in the year. *And* it's a good way to showcase the classroom library and let kids in on the titles that are available to them.

What about the configuration of kids' desks or tables?

Because I want to encourage conversation and collaboration, I arrange tables in ways that promote just that. I put two or three together, with four children seated around two tables or six around three. Have desks instead? They can be grouped together, too.

Often classroom desks, tables, and chairs are different heights or made from different materials. When that's the case, consider grouping together tables and desks that are the same height and made from the same materials. It's a much better look and feel than grouping wooden and Formica tables or desks together, or tables, desks, or chairs of different sizes, colors, and heights. Sometimes table heights can be adjusted, but not always. And then you'll need that special screwdriver that nobody seems to have seen for several years now.

Thinking About Room Arrangement

Once you've thought about questions like these, and you're clear about the areas you want and need, you can begin to think about physical space and room arrangement. One of the best ways to begin is to move as many of the desks, tables, chairs, boxes, and crates as you can out into the hall or at least over to one side of the room. Take some time to look objectively at the space you have; take a look at your notebook entries and think carefully about the kinds of spaces needed and where it makes the most sense for them to go.

Sometimes it's fun to work with a colleague—you can help each other move furniture *and* think together about how best to create environments that are based on and support what you believe about teaching and learning.

Anne Goudvis, coauthor with Stephanie Harvey of *Strategies That Work* (2007), and I did just that with an entire staff of teachers one summer—it's amazing what can happen in just a few days when you're focused! The first day we talked philosophy, and in the days that followed, teachers created spaces for teaching and learning that combined both form and function. It was really the Katy thing all over again, only on a much larger scale.

During this process, we had to get into what we called the "acceptance mode." In the beginning, there was talk of wanting round tables, square tables, desks, wall-to-wall carpeting, new trash cans, more space to display student work, custom-made shelves, more tubs and baskets for books, and strategies for getting rid of at least some of the huge (and permanent) chalkboards that lined classroom walls. Things like larger rooms, lofts, windows, and doors that lead outside were part of the conversation, too.

All these things would be lovely, but ultimately we had to face reality. In the end we had to work with what we had. And once the shift was made, teachers realized that teaching isn't so much about the shape of the tables, the carpet, or whether shelves are high or low. Good teaching, more than anything else, rests squarely with us.

And once it became all about us, teachers began to focus on what they did have rather than on what they didn't. Check out some of the innovative and brilliant ways they made the most of what they had (and got most of what they wanted) by making the following changes (see the color insert for the figures referred to in the following list):

- creating instant built-in shelves by taking the doors off cupboards (See Figure 3.2 in the color insert.)
- covering some of those huge chalkboards with sound-deadening board bought at home improvement stores like Home Depot. Now, teachers could use pushpins to secure anchor charts and student work rather than rolling all that masking tape and sticking it all over the back of things. No more coming in bright and fresh on Monday morning, only to find everything on the floor! (See Figure 3.3 in the color insert.)
- painting over existing bulletin boards. The fire marshal had been here, too, and teachers weren't allowed to back bulletin boards with paper or fabric. No problem! Paint was a perfect solution. We also found eight-by-ten-inch picture frames at the dollar store, and framed some of the student work in those and hung them on the bulletin boards. Teachers report that student work was easily inter-changed. (But check this out before you buy—some frames make changing easier than others.)
- bringing color to their rooms by painting furniture and bookshelves or using contact paper. (Any kids who wandered in and wondered what was going on were put to work!) (See Figure 3.3 in the color insert.)
- replacing old and rusty classroom trash cans with new ones bought with building maintenance money
- creating a common area for swapping furniture—say, desks for tables, low bookshelves for higher ones, easels for chart stands, and other things that one teacher didn't want but another might
- spraying pillows, rugs, and carpets with fire-marshal-approved fire retardant (this guy became our friend!)
- teachers making their wish lists known to parent and community groups; several parents got together and offered to make bookshelves for teachers who wanted them; others built lofts for the two kinder-garten rooms.

The principal of the school was savvy and smart. Not only did she help with the work, but she gave each teacher $125 to spend any way she wished on her classroom environments. *Now* was the time for those trips to Dollar Tree, Carpet Exchange, and Target!

A Grand Tour of everyone's classroom was held at the end of the third day. The rooms were spectacular; teachers buzzed about going on the road and calling their show Extreme Classrooms. But their principal brought them back to reality. She'd invested serious money into this project, and didn't want to lose them to fame and fortune just yet!

Katy Update

Because school was in session when Katy and I worked together, we were able to involve her kids in the process of organizing and arranging the room. Once the clutter was cleared, she talked with her students about her beliefs about teaching and learning, and her hopes for them as readers, writers, mathematicians, scientists, and citizens of the world.

She invited them to add their thinking to the discussion, and somehow, she tells me, this morphed into a discussion about passion; one child defined it as "What it is you like, love, and cherish; what it is that makes you, you."

They wanted their classroom to reflect their passions in some way; they wanted opportunities to explore them and share them with one another. These fifth graders shared their beliefs:

- Passions can help you believe in yourself and achieve your goals.
- Everyone is passionate about something—if you aren't right now, don't worry, something will come to you if you pay attention to yourself and listen.
- What if we didn't have any passions? We'd all be the same and that would be so boring.
- Sometimes passions can be driven away if we don't pay attention to them.

Subsequent discussions focused on room arrangement and organization, and ways to bring together Katy's ideas and those of her students. Small groups of interested kids were formed to create floor plans. Maps were drawn, pleas made, and, in the end, Katy and one member from each group made decisions about what the room would look like, complete with areas for pursuing passions. (More specifically, these were areas throughout the room housing science, social studies, writing, math, music, art books, and materials, but if they wanted to call them "passion places," well, hey, Katy went with it.)

Transformation Day was scheduled, and one Friday morning the room truly was transformed. Katy, her kids, and I pushed and pulled, stood and looked, and pushed and pulled some more. By 11:00 everyone gathered in the new and very spacious meeting area for punch and cookies. And to admire their organized, clean, cozy, and beautiful new room! (See Figure 3.4a, b, and c in the color insert.)

Thinking About Literate, Purposeful, Authentic Environments

Have you ever walked through a model home? The beds are meticulously made, the dining-room table is set for company, and everything is in its place. Decorators have done their best to give us the impression that someone actually lives here—there's the tennis racquet placed casually on the bed, a monogrammed terry-cloth robe hanging on a hook in the bathroom, and silver and gold foil-wrapped Hershey's kisses fill the candy dish. Everything, including the flowers, matches.

Let's say we come back in a week for another look. Guess what? The table's *still* set for company, bedspreads have nary a wrinkle, and everything's still in its place. In the real world, the tennis racquet would probably be stuffed somewhere in the closet by now, the robe coffee-stained and in the laundry basket, and there's *no way* that candy dish would still be filled with chocolate kisses.

So, what's up? What's missing? Missing are real people who lead real lives.

There's nothing authentic about environments like these. There's no way they really can be. Anybody (or nobody) could live inside these walls. There's no heart. There's no soul.

But classrooms are different. They're inhabited by real teachers and real kids who are learning interesting things, leading literate lives, and working hard to make meaning for themselves, each other, and their place in the world.

And that learning, those lives, and all that hard work need to be show-cased, front and center. Think back to our anchor classroom. Hardly anything was commercially made. We didn't see laminated posters of monkeys hanging from trees imploring us to "Hang in there! It's almost Friday!" No swarming honeybees urging us to "Bee sweet!" And no little red school-house on the front door, welcoming all who enter.

Instead, everything on those walls was purposeful and authentic. In just that brief glimpse, we had a clear sense of what that teacher and those kids were all about. Nobody told us. *Nobody had to.* That's because much of the teaching, learning, and *thinking* had been made visible, public, and permanent. We saw not only the evidence of learning, but also the processes students and their teacher used to get there.

And had I gone back a week later? I know for sure it wouldn't have looked the same. The changes would have been subtle—not a massive taking down and putting up—but I'm pretty certain I'd see children recording new learning on that huge Underground Railroad anchor chart, discovering more about how to go about selecting books for a variety of purposes, and referring to the *Librarian of Basra* anchor chart to apply the same process of determining importance independently in their own reading.

Thinking About Organizing Books and Materials

It used to be I was always looking for something in my classroom. Maybe it was that special pair of scissors, my attendance/grade book, or that long-overdue library copy of Cynthia Rylant's *The Journey, Stories of Migration*.

It was the same for my kids. I'd hear them calling out:

"Where's my writer's notebook? I left it right over there yesterday . . ."
"Does anybody know where the tape is?"
"I need an atlas—who moved them?"
"Where are all the Lemony Snickets?"
"Hey! We need more sticky notes!"

Now I know that when I'm always looking for things, when students and I can't put our hands on what we need when we need it, it becomes time-consuming and frustrating. Sometimes it's easier to give up and go on.

But giving up and going on doesn't lend itself to active teaching and learning. It's a passive stance that runs counter to developing those can-do, let-me-have-at-it kinds of attitudes I want for kids. When the mood or the need strikes, kids and I need to know just where to go to get what we need.

What can we do so that kids and teachers can put their hands on what they need when they need it? What might we do to not only *set the stage* for inquiry, understanding, and independence, but also begin to develop these ways of thinking in our students?

First, involving kids in the organization and placement of books and materials is a smart thing for us to consider. Kids will learn a thing or two about thoughtful organization, *and* because they've been part of the placement process, they'll know firsthand where things are kept, why it makes sense to keep them there, and where to put things back.

This makes me think of Ralph Peterson's reflections on classroom organization: "When a large number of people share a crowded place, productive life is possible only when the place is orderly" (1992, 63). But we can't stop there. We also need to discuss the why, the what for, and the how to.

Let's say we've stocked the writing area with paper, pencils, an electric pencil sharpener, markers, staplers, staples, and staple removers. We've put out the Wite-Out, paper punches, glue, and rubber cement. Paper clips, sticky notes, and pushpins are arranged in containers just the right size. Dictionaries and thesauruses stand tall on a bookshelf close by, alongside tubs holding mentor texts and the current author study.

"Hold on just a minute!" you might be thinking. "Wite-Out? Sticky notes? Staplers, paper clips, and rubber cement? Are you kidding? You really put those out? There's no way my kids will use them in the ways they were intended." If this is your response, I get it. I've personally known children who have created blinding snowstorms using an entire bottle of Wite-Out, made action-packed flip books out of packs of sticky notes, linked paper clips into lovely three-foot chains, and covered all ten fingers with glue or rubber cement, just for the fun and feel of peeling it off when it dries.

These behaviors are precisely why we have to model, discuss, and demonstrate why these things are in the writing area, what they are for, and how to use them. Once we show kids how to use materials throughout the room, we can trust them, and they can trust themselves, to use them in a variety of appropriate ways.

It's the same with books. I can organize them, put them into tubs, and thoughtfully place them throughout the room, but even that isn't enough. I also need to do book talks; teach kids the kinds of things they might expect when reading a certain series, author, or type of text; and teach them how to choose the books they'll read with purpose and intention.

How I decide to organize books and materials says a lot about the ways I see myself and my students. Because I want my kids to develop a sense of identity, to become problem posers and problem solvers, and see themselves as the kind of kids who can figure things out, they need access to a wide range of books and materials that allow them to do and be just that.

Sometimes teachers come back to school weeks before the kids are due. I was one of them. I couldn't seem to help myself—once August rolled around, I started thinking SCHOOL. I thought about the kids I'd have, big-picture planning, and the one thing I wanted to focus on as a teacher that year. (Would it be conferring? Writing workshop? Thinking strategies across the curriculum?)

But mostly, in those first few weeks, it was all about *the room*. Before I could begin to think seriously about planning or what I was most interested in learning more about that year, I had to get things in order. For me, it was a ritual, easing myself back into school, preparing the classroom, and my mind, for the days ahead.

But not all of us have that luxury, the need, or the time. And I learned from working with Katy that inviting and involving students in the process of organizing books and materials says a lot to them about what we believe about teaching and learning. It sends the message that we believe in kids and value their opinions; that the books and materials are *ours*; that this year their role in the classroom is going to be an active, participatory one.

For all you early birds out there, stay with me. We can come back to school whenever we want! But just maybe, after we've arranged the room in a way that feels right for now, we can hold off putting out and organizing *all* our books and materials. We want to be ready for the first days of school, with things like pencils, markers, scissors, notebooks, and glue organized and accessible, but what about involving the kids in some of the rest of it?

It does sound a little scary, but you have to trust that it's probably going to look much the way it would have had you done it yourself, except that now you've done some community building along the way, you've gotten some real help, *and* you and your kids know where things are. It might *sound* chaotic, but if we plan our work and work our plan, it doesn't have to be.

When kids walk into classrooms on the first day of school, we want them to feel, "Oh good! There's room for me here!" When everything is already done, kids don't have to wonder much about who is in charge. They know that from the minute they walk into the room.

That's why on the first days of school the classroom walls, bulletin boards, and doors will be almost bare. That's as it should be! Don't jump in and "put stuff up" just to make yourself feel better. Be patient. Wait. In a few days, your students' classroom portraits could be smiling back at you, beginning of the year interviews posted for all to see, and the Welcome to Our Classroom sign gracing your front door—kid-made and beautiful.

In the days, weeks, and months to come, those walls will fill with artifacts and learning that are unique to you and your students. It will reflect your stories and the stories of this year's group. You probably won't have an anchor chart about the book *The Librarian of Basra*, but then again, you might. Maybe you will highlight how making connections from your reading to the world enhances understanding. Or maybe it will be something else entirely. The point is, charts and student work reflect the teaching and learning in your classroom.

Classroom environments are organic—they grow as we do. The best of them reflect the hearts and souls of those who inhabit them. They're never really finished. They're never really "done." How could they be, when every day students and teachers learn something new?

CHAPTER 4

Creating Classroom Cultures That Support *and* Promote Student Thinking

Miss Miller I'd have never beeN a brillunt thiker. I am Now just From You.

love charles

Charles and the letter he wrote on the last day of first grade.

I believe we cannot underestimate the power of our influence—what we choose to say and do in the classroom profoundly affects the ways children view their teacher, themselves, and each other.

43

■ ■ ■ ■ ■ ■   A few summers back I worked for a couple of weeks with a group of teachers and kids in Junction City, Kansas. I was part of a summer school/professional development initiative there, where I'd teach a lesson with third and fourth graders in the afternoon and observing teachers would teach a similar lesson with their students the following morning.

Junction City in July can be hot, and at the end of one particularly scorching afternoon, I ask kids, "What do you do after school to cool down? I need some advice." Their recommendation? The Shaved Ice Stand.

"You're not gonna believe it," they tell me as they skip out the door. "You'll think you're in Hawaii!"

I'm tempted to jump in the car and drive over immediately, but on reflection I figure it will be packed with the parents and kids I said goodbye to just minutes before. I'm not quite ready for that, and besides, I have work to do.

Children and I were working on asking questions as we read and I'd been thinking aloud about my questions during read-alouds. I'd been using picture books, and kids were practicing by asking questions in self-selected picture books as well. At the end of the day, I'd often ask them to leave their books open to a page where they've recorded a question they believe to be important one. "Find a question you feel like you need to know the answer to in order to understand the big ideas in the story" I'd say to them, "and leave your books open to that page. At the end of the day I want to take a look at the kinds of questions you're asking—are you okay with that? Great! It'll help me figure out where we need to go next."

So I slip some quarters into the pop machine, grab a handful of goldfish crackers from the cupboard, slide something by Lyle Lovett into the CD player, and sit myself down in Dylan's chair. He's reading *The Story of Jumping Mouse*, a beautiful tale by John Steptoe about a little mouse whose hopeful and unselfish spirit leads him to the Far-Off Land, the land of his dreams.

Dylan's book is open to the page near the middle of the book, and I see he's written "Why does the author use such a powerful phrase?" on one blue sticky note and "Keep hope alive within you" on another (see Figure 4.1a, b).

Because I want to guide him as a reader the next day, I write back (on a sticky note, of course!) "Hi Dylan. Go back through the text today. When did John Steptoe use this phrase? What was happening? Why might it be important? Let me know! Mrs. Miller" (see Figure 4.1c).

Thirty or so minutes later I've written short notes to Dylan and four others, tidied up a bit, and posted the morning message. *Now* it's time to head over to the Shaved Ice Stand!

And it *is* amazing—tall palms decorated in tiny white lights, Adirondack chairs for resting, and delicious shaved ice. And truly, it's enough like Hawaii that I'm inspired to write this poem in my notebook.

FIGURES 4.1A, B, AND C

Kansas Cool
We stand in line
to spoon
shaved ice
under plastic palms.

Tangerine, banana,
sour cherry . . .
the possibilities
tickle our tongues.

But is it the ice
that brings us,
or the cicadas' song?

LOUD
ELECTRIC

Singing, screaming pretty,
each of us
together
one night
in Junction City

I think it's an okay poem, but when I take a minute to share it with the class the next day, *they* think it's so good that I should send it to the newspaper!

I pull up a chair beside Dylan later that morning, and confer with him briefly. "Hey, Dylan. I see you're rereading *The Story of Jumping Mouse*. What are you thinking about that phrase, 'Keep hope alive within you'? Have you figured out why the author used such a powerful phrase?"

"Well, I think so," he replies. "And I was wondering if, well, um, I was wondering if I could make a poem about it. Like, you know, the 'Kansas Cool' poem you wrote? Could I write about it like that?"

"You know what?" I say. "That's a great idea! I can't wait to see what you've figured out. And writing a poem about it? I love that."

Fifteen minutes later he comes to me, beaming from head to toe. "Want to hear it?" And he reads (see Figure 4.2).

"Wow," I tell him. "That's so good you should send it to the newspaper!"

When I think about myself early in my teaching career, I realize I wasn't a reflective reader or writer. I didn't keep a notebook with me and I wouldn't have thought to write a poem, much less share it with my kids. But when we believe we can write a poem at any moment and act on that belief, isn't it amazing how we can inspire can-do spirit in the children we teach?

When I think back to our anchor classroom and others like it, it's this same kind of spirit that permeates the very air. Children seem to breathe in, "I/We can do this" and breathe out, "Here's how." They see themselves and each other as kids with purpose; they see themselves as the kind of kids who can figure things out. These children sense that they have the capacity to

FIGURE 4.2

> "*Keeping Hope Alive*"
>
> The Jumping Mouse was "Keeping
> hope alive."
>
> He crossed a desert. He crossed a stream,
>   Keeping hope alive,
> He gave his sight, he gave his smell,
>   Keeping hope alive.
> He got to the far-away land, (his dream)
> Keeping Hope Alive!

roll up their sleeves, take action, and get things done. And wouldn't you know—the teacher sees herself, *and* them, that way, too? We see it in their faces. We witness it in their actions, their work, and their words. Peter Johnston (2004) might say that these children have developed a sense of "agency."

Creating classroom cultures that promote and support thinking and understanding does sound pretty lofty, doesn't it? But think back to our anchor classroom. Wasn't it just such a culture that children and their teachers were immersed in? So maybe *lofty* isn't the right word after all. Let's replace it with the word *essential*. Because if not for cultures like this one, I don't think I'd have

- met the three boys off in a distant corner, working together to synthesize *The Harmonica* in order to understand the story's big ideas;
- seen the huge chart along one wall showcasing student learning and thinking about the Underground Railroad, detailing not only the

learning but relevant vocabulary, student questions about this time and place in history, and their heartfelt responses;

■ witnessed children coming together and facilitating a discussion about what they learned about themselves as readers that day.

So what's going on here? How did kids and their teacher get to this place? How is it that they are such active teachers and learners, focusing their energy on thinking and understanding?

Remember earlier, when I wrote this about our anchor classroom?

My visit was in early April, but back in September, way before leaves began to fall or rain gave way to snow, I'm betting that classroom didn't look at all the way it does now. I'm betting those kids didn't sound or act the way they did the day I stepped inside. And I'm betting their teacher didn't either.

But the odds are good that she had a vision then of what she wanted for her kids in the weeks and months ahead, and that she's made conscious decisions and taken deliberate actions to get them there ever since. When teachers have a set of beliefs that guides our work, we know where we're going. There may be twists and turns along the way, but we always know where we're headed. When we know what we want for our kids in March, April, and May, we can set about getting them there starting in September.

Now that we've taken a look at room arrangement and organizing books and materials, let's shift our attention to another vital concern—creating cultures that support and promote student thinking. Let's set about the business of getting them there by considering the following:

■ putting our thinking on display;
■ the intentional use of language; and
■ making thinking visible, public, and permanent.

Remember the old teacher's tale about not smiling until Christmas? Don't believe it. The messages we send on the first days and weeks of school are the messages that set the tone for the entire year. From all the ways we put our thinking and theirs on display to what we say and do to foster and find significance in student thinking, we're letting kids in on who we are, what we expect from them (and ourselves), and what we believe about teaching and learning. And yes! A smile goes a long way, too.

Putting Our Thinking on Display

Our students are learning from us all the time. Ron Ritchhart, in *Intellectual Character: What It Is, Why It Matters, and How to Get It,* describes it this way:

> *One of the things they are learning (from us) is what thinking looks like. In thoughtful classrooms, a disposition toward thinking is always on display. Teachers show their curiosity and interest. They display open mindedness and willingness to consider alternative perspectives. Teachers model their own process of seeking truth and understanding. They show a healthy skepticism and demonstrate what it looks like to be strategic in one's thinking. They frequently put their own thinking on display and model what it means to be reflective. This demonstration of thinking sets the tone for the classroom, establishing both the expectations for thought and fostering students' inclination toward thinking.* (2002, 161)

This might sound a little lofty, too, but I think you'll find it's more attainable than you might believe. The following are some samples of words that model for our students what deep thinking looks like.

We're showing kids our curiosity and interest when we say things like this:

> *"Did you guys notice how close Venus was to the moon last night?" Or, "Remember yesterday when Erika brought in that black rock that we thought might be lava? I found a book that has a picture of a rock that looks just like hers—listen to this!" Or, "Look at that tree over there by the swings. The leaves are all dry and brown, but they're still hanging on. Why haven't they fallen off?"*

We're showing our open-mindedness and willingness to consider alternative perspectives when we say things like this:

"So you're thinking the boy let go of his dream at the end of The Sign Painter? *What leads you to believe that? Hmmm. I'm going to have to go back and look more closely at that part again. I was thinking he was going to keep following his dream, but now I'm not so sure. Thanks for getting me thinking, Ramon!"*

We're modeling our own "process of seeking truth and understanding" when we say things like this:

"Let's see here. At first I thought this book was about a librarian whose library was a meeting place for all who loved books. But when we read this page, now I'm thinking it's about so much more. When Alia Mohammed Baker realizes the war is coming to Basra and she asks the governor for permission to move the books to a safer place and he refuses, it says, 'So Alia takes matters into her own hands. Secretly, she bring books home every night, filling her car late after work.' Now I'm thinking The Librarian of Basra *is about a woman who loves books so much she's willing to risk her life to save them."*

We're modeling what it means to be reflective when we say things like this:

"Yesterday after school I did some thinking about our discussion of the Underground Railroad. Remember when some of you wondered, 'Why did some black people not want to escape on the Underground Railroad?' I'm wondering now if maybe it was because they didn't trust the conductors. Maybe they didn't believe the conductors were really going to help them to freedom."

And we're showing kids what it means to have healthy skepticism for the written and spoken word when we say things like this:

"Wow. Listen to this. Here it says that the queen ant lays over half a million eggs in her lifetime. Can that be true? That's a lot of

eggs! I'm going to check some other sources just to make sure—I think I read somewhere else that it was more like a hundred thousand . . ." Or, *"Caitlin, you said you heard on television that an ant can live in a jar of water for ten days. That seems almost unbelievable, doesn't it? You think so, too? How about seeing if you can do a little research on that, just to make sure they have their facts straight."*

Why is putting our thinking on display in these kinds of ways significant? When we want to cultivate dispositions for thinking in our students, we want to show them what good thinking sounds like, why it's important, and where it can lead us. Yes, we can *tell* them the importance of being curious or reflective, or even explicitly teach lessons focusing on attributes like these, but unless we also share our literate lives with children and think aloud to make our dispositions for thinking visible in authentic ways across the day and over time, it's unlikely to make a real difference.

Teachers who put their thinking on display are teachers who are present. When we're present, we're tuned in to our thinking and responsive to what's going on in the classroom and the world; we're actively seeking truth and understanding. We make our thinking visible to show students what we want for them; we're showing them how being curious, thoughtful, and reflective enhances and enriches who we are as active teachers, learners, and citizens of the world.

It's important to know that even if you don't think of yourself as a particularly reflective person or someone who naturally puts your thinking on display, it doesn't mean it's not within you. I know, because I remember a time when I didn't think about myself that way either. It was as if I was so busy doing the *stuff* of teaching that I didn't have *time* to be thoughtful and reflective.

I kept my kids busy, too. If you had peeked into my room back then, you'd have probably thought all was well. You'd have seen children doing lots and lots of stuff. (Isn't it amazing how much alike my students and I were?) But had you looked more closely at *what* children were doing, you might have wondered what this busyness was really all about.

And now I wonder, could it be that I kept myself and my kids so busy because I didn't really know *what else* we should or could be doing? Was I avoiding an inconvenient truth of my own?

Looking back, I'd say the answer is yes. Being busy kept me from confronting what I was afraid to admit all along—I knew there was more to teaching but I didn't know what it was. I had the best of intentions. I wanted to be a good teacher. But I was looking outside myself for all the answers. I didn't know that most of the answers were already inside me. And I hope you know they're inside you, too.

I was so busy *managing* the classroom—keeping kids focused and moving them through activities—that to sit down next to a child and not only ask him how things were going, but take time to listen carefully and respond in a meaningful way was something I couldn't fathom finding time to do. And even if I'd found the time, I don't think that back then I'd have known what to say.

If I'm always rushing around, looking ahead to what's coming up next, I don't have the time, the inclination, or the mind-set to put my thinking on display. I used to think it was a luxury to be curious, thoughtful, and reflective.

Now I know being curious, thoughtful, and reflective is a necessity. When I'm teaching, I can't be thinking about the emergency faculty meeting after school, stopping at the cleaners on the way home, or running down the checklist of things I need for an upcoming science experiment. I can't be looking at the clock every few minutes thinking about what's next. I have to be actively engaged in what's happening now, at this precise moment.

How did I make this leap of faith? How did I go from managing a classroom to creating a classroom community responsive to student needs and interests, a classroom focused less on activities and more on thinking and understanding?

Many of us are now familiar with comprehension strategies proficient readers use to enhance understanding and construct meaning. We're aware that researchers spent a decade investigating what proficient readers do to comprehend text, what less successful readers fail to do, and what teachers might do to bring novices to expertise.

From this thinking synthesized by Pearson, Roehler, Dole, and Duffy (1992), we've learned that active, thoughtful readers use just a handful of comprehension strategies, including these:

- activating their prior knowledge and making connections between what they know and new information they encounter in the texts they read

- drawing inferences from the texts they read to form conclusions, make critical judgments, and create unique interpretations
- asking questions of themselves, the authors they encounter, and the texts they read
- determining the most important ideas and themes in a texts they read
- summarizing and synthesizing information within and across texts
- monitoring the adequacy of their understanding
- creating visual and other sensory images during and after reading

It was this work that created the shift for me. In order to teach my students how to go about using comprehension strategies like these in flexible and adaptive ways, I had to make my thinking visible. And to do that honestly and authentically, I had to relax, slow down, and be present. I had to learn how to become reflective on my feet, in the moment.

It was a tall order. Think out loud about my thinking? Actually *tell* kids when I didn't understand something? Expect the same from them? Well, yes. In time and with practice I learned to trust myself. I stopped worrying about whether my thinking was worthy or "right"; I came to understand that being authentic is what matters most. Now I know that being me was all I needed to be.

And even back then, back when putting my thinking on display wasn't something I did naturally, children began to say things that made me sit up and take notice. My words, however tentative, were coming back to me through them. My kids were learning to relax, slow down, and be present, too. (Isn't it amazing how much alike my students and I were?) And this time, had you looked closely at what they were saying and doing, you wouldn't have wondered what they were all about. It would have been abundantly clear.

The Intentional Use of Language

Peter Johnston, in his thought-provoking book *Choice Words: How Our Language Affects Children's Learning* (2004), writes

Teachers play a critical role in arranging the discursive histories from which children speak. Talk is the central tool of their trade. With it they mediate children's activity and experience, and help them make sense of learning, literacy, life, and themselves. (4)

When Peter says that talk is the central tool of a teacher's trade, he's not talking just any old talk. He's talking about the intentional ways we use language to help make meaning and attach importance to what children say and do.

Through language we send messages in subtle and sometimes not-so-subtle ways. I could simply tell students that I'm honored to be their teacher, that I think they're capable and smart, and that I trust them to make wise decisions, but unless I'm specific in my praise and my actions support my words, they might not hold much meaning.

For example, I could say, "What a thoughtful conversation we had today." But if I leave it at that, some children might wonder, "So what was thoughtful about it? Is she just saying that?" But what if I follow that statement with something like this:

"I loved the way we listened to each other and responded in ways that were respectful and took us in new directions today. Like did you notice when Makayla directed her comment to Sam, she didn't just repeat what Sam had said, or say, 'I think that, too'? She looked right at him, said his name, and connected her new thinking to his, taking our conversation deeper."

Children know exactly what I mean when I say, "What a thoughtful conversation we had today."

I want to elevate children in their own eyes as well as in the eyes of their classmates whenever I can. Noticing and naming thoughtful language and positive behaviors is one way to do that.

To make meaning and attach importance to what children say and do, we have to (once again and always!) be present. This can be tricky. When we're thinking out loud about our thinking when we're reading, we can, if we like, plan ahead where in the text we'll think aloud and even write on a sticky note what we want to say. But when we bring children into the mix, when we ask them to share their understanding, there's no way we can plan for or script a meaningful and authentic response ahead of time.

But we can plan to be present. We can plan to listen carefully, make sense of what the child has to say for ourselves, and respond in thoughtful and purposeful ways that acknowledge, clarify, honor, and support their efforts and move them forward.

Teacher Talk

We've all been in situations like the ones described in the following examples. Here are some ways to respond honestly and with caring the next time we find ourselves in these positions.

Let's say a child says something in response to a statement or question and we're not sure where they're headed.

If we smile, nod encouragingly, and say things like the following, we're letting children know we believe they have something significant to say and we're going to do everything we can to help them find it:

- Keep going.
- What else?
- Keep talking. I think you are onto something here.
- Say more about that.

It takes time to help children find words for what they're trying to convey. It can be uncomfortable. But when kids understand we're not going to ask them to do something unless we know they can do it, they most often accept our challenge.

Sometimes, when a child is having difficulty putting his thinking on display, we might say something like, "Is there anybody who can help Josh?" Lots of kids will want to help Josh, but will they really be able to? More than likely it's an opportunity for them to share their own thinking, and Josh learns that if he hesitates to answer, his teacher and his classmates will come to his rescue. That's no way to move a child forward.

So don't let Josh off the hook. Stick with him. Nod, smile, and say, "Keep talking, Josh." And then wait. Let him know you know that thinking takes time. Let him know that you truly believe he has something thoughtful to say. When children know we believe in them, it's the first step in learning to believe in themselves.

Let's say a child actually has quite a bit to say, but we're not really sure what she's talking about.

In this instance, we try as best we can to make sense of what she has to say and make meaning for ourselves. We're showing kids we really do want to understand their words and ideas when we say things like this:

- So, are you saying . . . ?
- Is this what you mean?
- This is what I think I heard you say. Do I have it right?

We try our best to find that golden nugget—to find significance—in what they have to say, and offer it up for the child's consideration.

How do we know what to say after saying something like, "So, is this what you mean?" (Especially when we have no clue?) Take a deep breath, think about the child's words, the focus of the discussion or conference, and say something that makes sense to you.

We don't really know if this is what the child is thinking, but we're having a go at it. It's important that we frame our understanding in the form of a question. "Is this what you mean?" sends a much different message from, "This is what you mean."

If the child answers with a nod or a yes, I say, "Okay. Now you say it." We're giving the child the opportunity to put it in her own words—she owns the thinking now. Sometimes I'm asked, "So how do you know she was really thinking that? How do you know she's not just *saying* that's what she was thinking?"

I don't. And I don't think it matters. What does matter is that the child understands that her teacher is working hard to make sense of what she has to say. And if we do end up giving her an out? So be it. Sometimes we forget that when we dismiss a child's thinking, we also dismiss the child. And conversely, when we embrace her thinking, we're also embracing her. We cannot underestimate the power of our influence.

Other times a child will say, "No, I'm not thinking that. I'm thinking this . . ."

Perfect. Either "Yes! I'm thinking that" or "No, I'm not thinking that, I'm thinking this . . ." helps children clarify their thinking. What we say and how we say it lets them know that it's safe to put their thinking on display.

Sometimes children say things that seem so bizarre (to us) that we wonder if they have been listening at all.

Instead of asking them that question, or giving them that special look we reserve for occasions just like these, we could decide to not pass judgment. We're being honest and we're showing kids that even though we've never thought about it quite like that before, we're willing to now when we say something like this:

■ Wow. I never thought about it like that before!

But what if children say things just to get a reaction from everyone? In that case, children know that we're open to listening to a variety of perspectives and ideas, and that we expect them to substantiate their thinking in thoughtful ways for themselves and others when we say something like this:

"So help me out here. What's the evidence in the text that leads you to draw this conclusion?" Or, "What in your experience makes you think about it in this way?"

Once students find out *we're* serious, that we're going to keep at it in order to find significance in what they have to say, they usually stop responding in less than thoughtful ways.

Sometimes we see that students need to broaden and expand their thinking and to value and make efforts to understand thinking that's different from their own.

We're helping children understand the importance of being open-minded, listening carefully, and learning from each other when we say things like this:

- What might be another way of thinking about this?
- Who has another point of view?
- Now let's look at this a different way. What if . . . ?
- Turn and talk with a partner about your thinking.

Children sometimes struggle to figure something out that's causing them difficulty.

We can send messages that say, "I believe in you. I believe you're capable. I don't doubt that you can do this, and I don't want you to doubt yourself either":

- So what's your plan?
- What do you think you'll do next?
- Have you had this kind of problem before? What did you do then?
- I can't wait to see how you'll figure this out!

It's important that we use language like this with all students. We can offer more or less support, depending on children's needs, but we want every one of them to believe that what we are asking them to do is within their reach. It's the first step in making it so.

And of course, we have to know our children well to make certain that it is. If we say, "I can't wait to see how you figure this out!" and they have no tools for the figuring, our words are more harmful than helpful. But if we've taught students a variety of strategies for constructing meaning and enhancing understanding and we're responsive to what they say and do, kids begin to believe that they're the kind of kid who can figure things out.

We might be inclined to tell a child what to do. It takes less time in the short run and is often easier. But what about the next time the child encounters a similar problem? Will she remember what we told her in the long run? Maybe. But if we're always telling, when will she ever learn to breathe in, "I can do this" and breathe out, "here's how"?

Think about this quote from Jean Piaget:

Each time one prematurely teaches a child something he could have discovered himself, that child is kept from inventing it and consequently from understanding it completely. (1983)

And when children make sense of something that's been puzzling them, we can let them know that we value, and we want them to value, the mental processes they use to construct meaning.

- How did you figure that out?
- What exactly did you do?
- What did you do that helped you most? What did you do that helped you the least?
- What did you learn about yourself as a reader (or writer, or mathematician, or scientist) today?
- I'm not sure everybody knows this. Would you be willing to share this with everyone when we come back together?

If nobody ever asks, they may not even be aware of what they did to figure things out. They may think it was just some lucky happenstance. We know that it wasn't, and we want them to know that, too, so that the next time they encounter difficulty, they can think back and say, "Oh! I've had this same kind of problem before, so I'll try . . ."

This kind of language encourages students to be metacognitive, to think about their thinking. And because we value their expertise, we want them to articulate what they did so others can learn from them. It's one thing to think to yourself about what you did and how you did it, and quite another to articulate that process to others. I want students to learn to do both.

☑ Something to Try

Over the next few weeks, become aware of the language you use with your students. What are the words or phrases you hear yourself using over and over? What do you notice about the kinds of things you say? Ask yourself:

- How do I position myself (physically and otherwise) in the classroom?
- How do I position my students?
- Do my words represent what I believe about teaching and learning? If not, how might I change them?

Making Thinking Visible, Public, and Permanent

When it comes to creating cultures of thinking, David Perkins—currently senior professor of education at the Harvard Graduate School of Education and a founding member of Project Zero—is the man. In an article titled "Making Thinking Visible," he writes,

> *Consider how often what we learn reflects what others are doing around us. We watch, we imitate, we adapt what we see to our own styles and interests, we build from there. Now imagine learning to dance when the dancers around you are all invisible. Imagine learning a sport when the players who already know the game can't be seen. Bizarre as this may sound, something close to it happens all the time in one very important area of learning: learning to think. Thinking is pretty much invisible. To be sure, sometimes people explain the thoughts behind a particular conclusion, but often they do not. Mostly, thinking happens under the hood, within the marvelous engine of our mindbrain.*
>
> *Fortunately, neither others' thinking nor opportunities to think need to be as invisible as they often are. As educators, we can work to make thinking much more visible than it usually is in classrooms. When we do so, we are giving students more to build on and learn from. By making the dancers visible, we are making it much easier to learn to dance.* (2003)

I believe that thinking aloud about our thinking is the best way to make thinking visible. And once children begin to put their thinking on display, have you ever wished that you could somehow capture the amazing things they say? Have you wondered how to make student thinking not only visible, but public and permanent as well? And do it in an authentic way?

I remember times during whole-group, small-group, and one-on-one discussions with children when I'd say to myself, "I wish this were on tape!" Or later in the day thinking, "Now what did Josh say about that? What were his exact words?" I'd remember the gist, but when I'd try to re-create his part of the conversation, my words didn't do Josh's words justice. In my re-creation, I'd lost the essence of Josh.

In our anchor classroom, evidence of student thinking was everywhere; anchor charts, student responses, and quotes adorned the walls and boards, making thinking public and permanent. Remember how the walls spoke to us? The questions, quotes, ideas, and big understandings displayed throughout the room reflected the real voices of real kids.

Why is making thinking public and permanent in our classrooms a smart thing for us to do? It lets students know that thinking matters. When children are immersed in classroom cultures where thinking is well documented, it reminds students of the results of past endeavors and invites and encourages new ones.

We honor children and their thinking when we capture it precisely. Whether we're creating an anchor chart, recording quotes for display, or using a child's words to frame a discussion, authenticity is essential. If we choose to "fix their thinking up" to mirror our own, or try to remember it later, the meaning is inevitably changed and the thinking ceases to be theirs. But other than webcasting our classrooms seven hours a day, what might be a practical way for teachers to capture student thinking and make it public and permanent?

I keep a notebook with me when I teach. It's unobtrusive and small, no larger than six by nine inches, and it fits easily on my lap or a nearby chalk ledge or table. I don't record everything, of course, but when children say something that seems particularly insightful or poignant, I want to capture their words exactly as they said them. And put it up for all to see. A notebook is perfect for that.

We might not want to take the time then and there to write it up and make it public, but we've made it permanent in our notebooks so that when we, or the children, have time, we can.

It's the same with anchor charts. Maybe we're learning about how readers determine what's important in their reading, and I want to create an anchor chart that reflects our thinking and understanding. If I record what children say in my notebook during the lesson, I can create an anchor chart later that is accurate and authentic. *The Harmonica* chart is an example of an anchor chart constructed in this way (see Figure 4.3). Depending on my purposes, I also create charts like these during the lesson, but it's nice to have options.

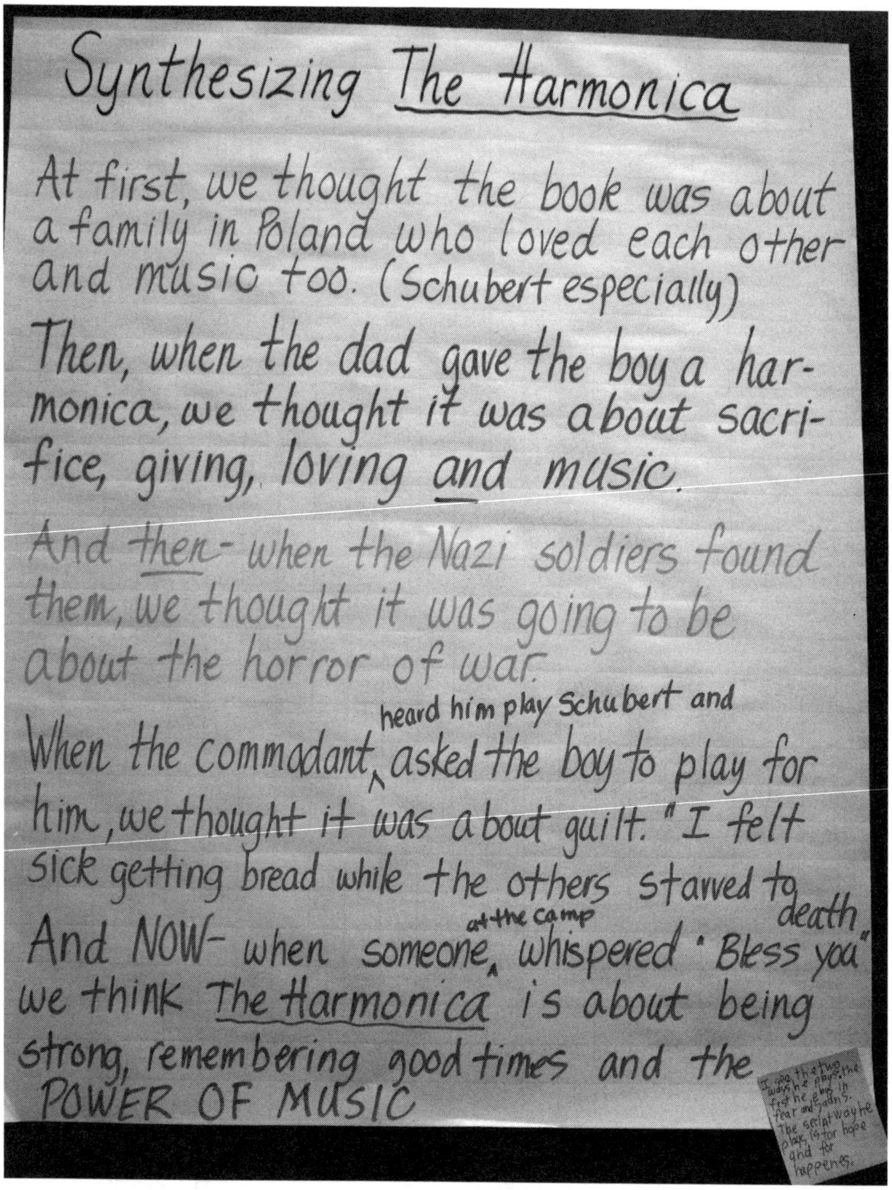

FIGURE 4.3
Anchor charts make thinking
and learning visible, public,
and permanent.

> # Synthesizing The Harmonica
>
> At first, we thought the book was about a family in Poland who loved each other and music too. (Schubert especially)
>
> Then, when the dad gave the boy a harmonica, we thought it was about sacrifice, giving, loving and music.
>
> And then— when the Nazi soldiers found them, we thought it was going to be about the horror of war.
>
> When the commandant heard him play Schubert and asked the boy to play for him, we thought it was about guilt. "I felt sick getting bread while the others starved to death.
>
> And NOW— when someone at the camp whispered "Bless you" we think The Harmonica is about being strong, remembering good times and the POWER OF MUSIC

You may think that keeping track of thinking in a notebook while teaching sounds awkward and time-consuming. Maybe that's true in the beginning, but in time and with practice, it becomes as natural as thinking aloud. Even now, when I'm working in classrooms with children who are not my own, I always make sure I have my notebook with me.

After introducing myself and letting kids know how happy I am to be with them this day, I often ask, "So what do you know that readers do?" I record their responses and names in my notebook, sometimes asking, "So are you saying . . . ," "Tell me more about that," "How does that help you as a reader?" or "What do you understand *now* (after rereading, asking questions, making connections, etc.) that you didn't understand before?"

Documenting student thinking is such a simple act, and yet I believe it sets the tone for our time together. Right away, students know I value what they know and who they are. Just like language, it's another important tool of my trade.

CHAPTER 5

Swimming *with* Sharks: Teaching *for* Understanding *and* Engagement

I believe learning is maximized when the lessons I design are purposeful, interactive, and engaging, with real-world applications.

■ ■ ■ ■ ■ ■ ■

Good morning, everyone!" I say to the twenty-six second graders sitting on the floor before me. I'm in Valerie Burke's classroom in Denver, just down the hall and across the way from the room where I used to teach.

I introduce myself, let children know how happy I am to be working with them over the next few days, and ask them to share a bit about the kinds of things they know that readers do.

"Listen to you," I tell them, reading their responses from my notebook: "rereading, making connections, reading lots of different kinds of books, sounding out words, asking questions—you already know so much!

"In our time together over the next few days we're going to be learning even more about the kinds of things that readers do. Some of the things we'll be talking about will be familiar to you; other things might be new. But don't worry—I'm not going to ask you to do anything I don't think you can do. Are you ready?"

A few skeptics look over at their teacher, Mrs. Burke. But all it takes is a nod and a smile from Valerie, and we're good to go.

"Today we're going to be doing some work with nonfiction. Let's begin by thinking together about the kinds of things you've come to expect when you read this type of text. When you read nonfiction, what are some of the things you can almost always count on? What are some things you already know about this type of text?"

Children respond, and I record in my notebook.

- It's about real stuff, and it's true/Jaime
- There will be lots of facts/Chloe
- You'll see photographs, and cutaways and a table of contents/Shyann

"Wow!" I say. "You know a lot about nonfiction already. And here's something else I'd like you to think about: When you read nonfiction, would you say that you can almost always count on learning something new? Would you say you can almost always count on learning something you didn't know before?

"You would? I think so, too.

"But here's a problem I have, and I'm wondering if this ever happens to you. Have you ever been reading a great nonfiction text that's full of important information? Maybe it's a magazine, a book, or one of your text-books. Maybe it's even something you learned online or while watching The Discovery Channel. Then another day you're talking with a friend, or your mom or dad, or your teacher, and you want to tell them all about what you read, or saw, or heard, only you can't remember what you learned?

"That happens to you, too? Whew! I'm glad I'm not the only one. Today and tomorrow we're going to work together to learn some specific things we can do to help us understand and remember new learning."

The Thinking Behind the Teaching

When Valerie and I were collaborating about our work together, I learned that she and her kids were in the midst of a nonfiction study in reading and writing—kids were reading and writing exclusively nonfiction and had most recently been learning about its features and conventions. They'd just completed their Nonfiction Convention Notebooks (see Miller 2002) and were applying what they'd learned in their daily reading and writing workshops.

In science they'd been studying sea creatures, and they were just beginning a study of sharks. I'd have known even if she hadn't told me—baskets of shark books sat atop clusters of tables where children worked, filled with books at a variety of levels that included the following titles:

- *My Best Book of Sharks* by Claire Llewellyn
- *Hunting Sharks* by Kristin Nelson
- *100 Things You Should Know About Sharks* by Steve Parker
- *Sharks and Other Dangers of the Deep* by Simon Mugford
- *Life-Size Sharks and Other Underwater Creatures* by Daniel Gilpin
- *See-Through Sharks* by Stephen Savage
- *Shark Attack!* by Cathy Dubowski
- *What Do Sharks Eat for Dinner?* by Melvin and Gilda Berger
- *Hungry, Hungry Sharks!* by Joanna Cole
- *Sharks* by Seymour Simon
- *Shark* (Eyewitness Books) by Miranda Macquitty
- *Sharks! TIME for Kids* Science Scoops series by the editors of *TIME for Kids*

Each basket (five altogether) had multiple copies of *Hunting Sharks* and *Hungry, Hungry Sharks!*—Valerie knew all her kids could read these titles easily and glean new information from them. The other titles were interspersed throughout the baskets, and though she knew many of these would be difficult for children to decode, she also understood (brilliant teacher that she is!) that the photographs, captions, cutaways, comparisons, and the huge fold-out life-size shark jaws (*Life-Size Sharks*) would make these more difficult texts accessible and give kids an opportunity to apply what they'd learned about nonfiction conventions. Not to mention that the books she'd chosen were perfect for engaging kids, getting them talking *and* building background knowledge!

As Valerie and I talked, I learned that her kids loved reading nonfiction (they couldn't wait to get their hands on those shark books) but that when she conferred with them and asked about what they'd learned, she was noticing they were having difficulty remembering and understanding what they'd read.

I could relate! In *Reading with Meaning* (2002) I wrote briefly about a Mental Files lesson I'd designed with my first graders in mind—I'd wanted to make visible the process of activating, building, and revising schema in order to help them remember and understand new learning; they had been experiencing some of the same difficulties Valerie's kids were.

And that got me thinking. How might Valerie and I take that lesson and adapt and expand it to meet the needs of these second graders? How might we teach kids strategies for remembering and understanding new learning in nonfiction by making schema theory—connecting new learning to what we already know—even more concrete?

We decided to make a file similar to the one I wrote about in *Reading with Meaning*, only this one would be bigger and better. What comes next is the lesson in its entirety. We worked through it with the kids over two days. I share it with you not because I'm hoping you'll turn around and do it with your kids. You could, of course, but that's not my purpose. The point isn't about finding the perfect lesson or progression of lessons to follow exactly. The point is to know who you are and what you're about when you're teaching based on your beliefs, your students, and the environment you are creating. Once we define our beliefs, align our practices, and know our children and the curriculum well, we can create purposeful lessons at any time that make sense and meet our children's needs precisely.

And now that we're not rushing around all the time anymore (right?), we might be able to find some quiet moments at the end of the day to think about where we've been with our kids, where we are now, and where it makes the most sense to go next.

When analyzing lessons, you might ask yourself the following questions:

- How does this lesson fit with what children and I are already doing? How will it take the learning further?
- Will it engage students? How are teachers and students positioned for teaching and learning? Is thinking valued and made visible? Is there student input? Is independence on the radar?
- What happens after the lesson? Will students be given time for practice and feedback from me? How else will they be supported? How will I know they understand?
- What might some of the implications be for learning in the days and weeks to come?

Because, as Frank Smith says, "We can only learn from activities that are interesting and comprehensible to us; in other words, activities that are satisfying. If this is not the case, only inefficient rote-learning, or memorization, is available to us and forgetting is inevitable" (1998, 87).

So, let's get to the lesson.

"Girls and boys, let's think about it this way today. Inside our brains we have lots and lots of mental files. Do you know what files are? Okay. So we have these files, and they are filled with all the things we know about. Maybe you call it your schema, or your background knowledge. Like you probably have a brainfile for dinosaurs, one for math, a soccer file . . . can you think of others? Get eye-to-eye and knee-to-knee and talk with each other about some of the files you have inside your head.

"See? In our brains we have lots and lots of mental files where we store all the things we believe to be true. We're always adding new information to our files, and because there's so much to learn, we have to try to figure out how to remember and understand all that new learning, especially the things that are most important to us."

"It sounds kind of like we have a computer inside our heads," Raul offers. "A computer has millions of files, and you can add stuff to them, and make new ones, too."

Heads nod, and we all think that's a great way to think about it.

"So we have all this new learning and we want to remember it and deepen our understanding of how things work in the world. One of the best ways to do that is to make connections between new learning and what we already know.

"Because I know that in science you're learning about sea creatures, and sharks in particular, I'm thinking that you have a file inside your brain—like a computer file—that's filling up with information about sharks, right? So what we want to do, before we even begin to read this great book I brought, is to activate, or open up those files.

"Yep, Raul, it *is* like scrolling up and down and finding the file and pushing 'open' on the computer. When we do that, when we open up that file and think about our schema, or what we already know about sharks, we'll have something to connect our new learning to. Making those connections will help us understand and remember what we've learned. Everybody, shall we see how this works for us?"

Materials

I've made a huge file folder by using a large piece of poster board, cutting it in half and laminating it, leaving about a third of an inch between the two pieces so that it can be easily be folded in half, like a real file.

The file can be taped to the chalkboard or affixed to a chart stand, and formatted with the kids. Explaining and formatting the file takes a bit of time, but once it's done and kids understand the process, it can be reused and you can proceed much more quickly the next time.

Other materials include:

- a pack of three-by-three-inch sticky notes, any color (to record what we think we know);
- several packs of three-by-three-inch sticky notes of a *different* color (to record new learning);
- black Sharpie pens for you and the kids (these help make the writing easier to see and read);
- a variety of books on the topic, with a small pack of seven or eight sticky notes (the same color as the *different* color) placed on the cover of each book for children to record their new learning and questions.

Organizing the File

To begin, we label the front of the file "Sharks."

"Now," I say, opening the file and pointing to the top half, "here's where we're going to record all the things we think we know about sharks. Let's label this: Our Schema—What We Think We Know.

"On the bottom half of our file, here, let's write New Learning—this is where we'll record things we didn't know before. And down here, at the bottom right, let's write Misconceptions. Do you know that word?

"No? Misconceptions are those things that we once believed to be true, but when we read or hear new information we find out that they aren't true after all. Like I used to think the sun revolved around the earth. But that was a big misconception. Now I know that the earth revolves around the sun. You see? I had to take the information about the sun revolving around the earth out of my files, and replace it with my new learning—the earth revolves around the sun."

Computer whiz Raul calls out, "Hey! That's just like deleting! You just push a button in your brain and poof! Away it goes!"

And I say in my quietest voice, "You know what? I never really thought about it like that before, but that's just what it's like, and exactly what we want to do. Do you see what you are doing, Raul? You're making connections all over the place between what you already know about computers and the information I'm teaching you! You're doing the very thing we're talking about. You're making connections between something you already know about—computers—and new learning—mental files. That is just what readers do.

"All of us have probably had misconceptions at one time or another—that's just the nature of living and learning. But when we are faced with evidence that shows us that what we once believed to be true isn't true at all, it's the smart and brave person who lets go of the old thinking, and *deletes* it, just like Raul said, from their mental files. It's not part of what they know to be true anymore."

"So the new learning knocks out what's not true?" another child asks.

"That's it exactly," I say.

"Now that our file is ready to go, let's see how this theory works for us as we learn more about sharks. Let's do a little research ourselves and see if making connections between our new learning and what we already know helps us remember and understand. So open up those shark files, everyone, and let's record some of the things that you already know about sharks."

Researching

Children respond (see the list that follows), and I record each response on a sticky note, placing them on the top part of the file, under the label Our Schema—What We Think We Know.

- A shark is a fish.
- Sharks aren't fish.
- Sharks breathe through gills.
- If sharks stop moving, they will die.
- They're a little bit like whales.
- Sharks have rough skin.
- When sharks lose a tooth, they grow a new one.
- They have a powerful bite/they could bite your head off.
- Lantern sharks have glowing eyes, like a flashlight!
- Sharks eat other fish.
- There are lots of different kinds of sharks.

Next, I read aloud portions of Seymour Simon's *Sharks*, stopping to record new learning—some mine for modeling purposes, but mostly that of students—on the different-colored sticky notes and place them under the appropriate headings on the bottom half of the file folder.

For example, when I read, "Like most fish, sharks breathe through gills. But while most fish have one pair of gills, sharks have five to seven . . . ," I put the book down and say, "Did you hear that? Wow. I never knew sharks had that many pairs of gills!

"When you hear that little voice inside your head saying things like 'Whoa! Wow! That's amazing! Oh my gosh! Really?' or 'I never knew that before,' slow down, listen carefully, and think about what you just read. Reread it if you need to. Listening to what that little voice inside your head has to say is one way your brain signals you that this is new information, or new learning.

"So now I want to record this new learning to help me remember it, but of course I don't want to just copy it from the book, right? I want to put what I've just learned in my own words, writing down what's impor-

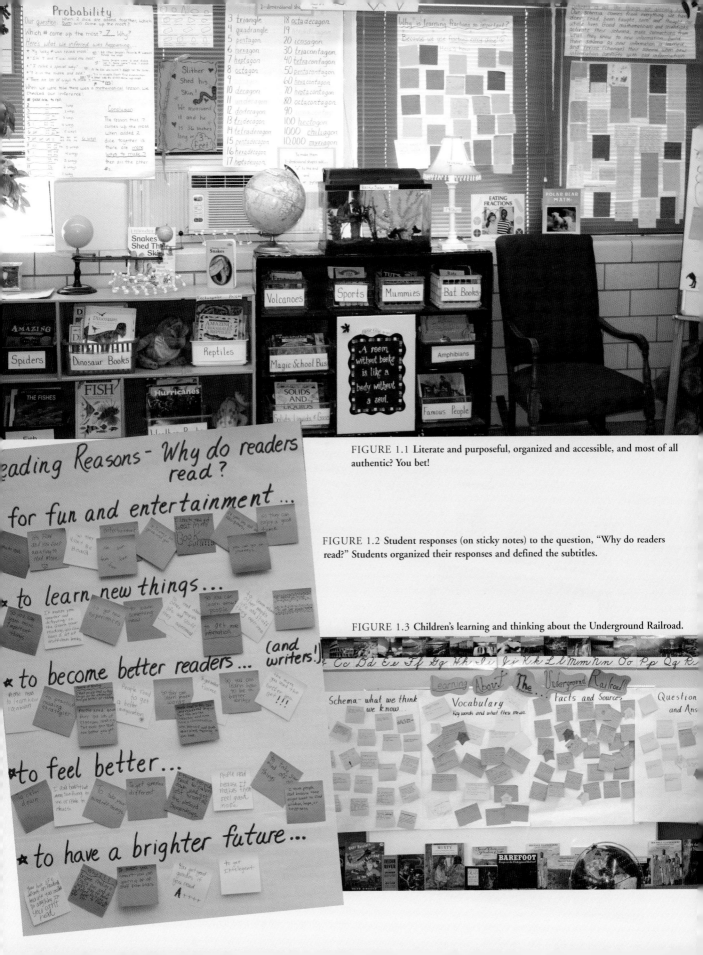

FIGURE 1.1 Literate and purposeful, organized and accessible, and most of all authentic? You bet!

FIGURE 1.2 Student responses (on sticky notes) to the question, "Why do readers read?" Students organized their responses and defined the subtitles.

FIGURE 1.3 Children's learning and thinking about the Underground Railroad.

FIGURE 3.2 Create added shelf space by removing cupboard doors.

FIGURE 3.3 Create bulletin boards for children's work, anchor charts, and more by covering large, unused chalkboards or blank walls with sound-deadening board and painting its surface. And how about that beautiful, newly painted table?

FIGURE 3.4A Katy and Debbie love what they see!

FIGURES 3.4B, C Katy's newly organized (and beautiful) room. Now *everybody* knows where their things are! Check out the seat pockets, caddies for pencils, glue, and sticky notes, etc., and tables arranged to promote conversation and collaboration.

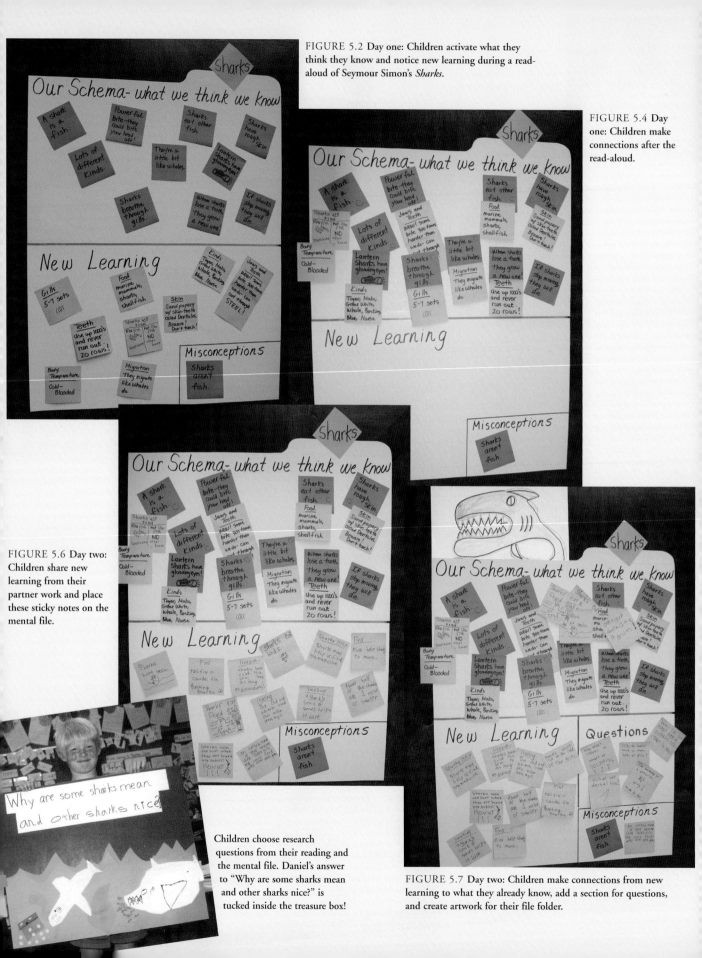

FIGURE 5.2 Day one: Children activate what they think they know and notice new learning during a read-aloud of Seymour Simon's *Sharks*.

FIGURE 5.4 Day one: Children make connections after the read-aloud.

FIGURE 5.6 Day two: Children share new learning from their partner work and place these sticky notes on the mental file.

Children choose research questions from their reading and the mental file. Daniel's answer to "Why are some sharks mean and other sharks nice?" is tucked inside the treasure box!

FIGURE 5.7 Day two: Children make connections from new learning to what they already know, add a section for questions, and create artwork for their file folder.

FIGURE 5.1

tant, in a way that makes sense to me, without telling too much. If I can do that, I know I understand it.

"I'm going to write the word 'Gills' with a line under it for the heading of my sticky note, like this, and under it I'll write five to seven sets—I think I'll even draw them, like this—and that's all I really need to do to help me remember. [See Figure 5.1.] Now I'll put this sticky note in our file, right under New Learning, just like this."

When we get to the part that reads "Sharks are fish, but they are very different from most fish," I stop. "Hmmm. This is important. Remember when some of us thought sharks were fish and some of us thought they weren't? Let's keep reading because I think this is going to help us get to the bottom of this."

We learn that like all fish, sharks have backbones and teeth, but unlike other fish they don't have any other bones. Their skeletons are made of cartilage instead.

"So now, everybody, let's think about this. Are sharks fish? Let's reread this paragraph and then turn and talk with each other about your thinking."

In the end we agree that they are, but that they have some important differences.

"So if you were thinking that sharks aren't fish, you'll want to get that information out of what you know to be true. Can you delete it right now? You can? Perfect! That's just what we're learning that readers do.

FIGURE 5.3
Two-column notes: how sharks are like fish and not like fish.

"Now let's take this sticky note, the one that says, 'Sharks are not fish,' and take it out of Our Schema and put it here, right under Misconceptions. Some of us thought that was true, but now we know it isn't, right? What we're doing here is just the way it works inside our brains. We're deleting it from our brainfiles. We're knocking it right out of there!" Figure 5.2 in the color insert shows what our file looks like at this point.

"Are there two of you who would like to get together right now and show in pictures and/or words how sharks are like and unlike fish? Thanks!" See Figure 5.3 for children's thinking on this matter.

I'm doing all I can in this lesson to make the comprehension process visible to Valerie's kids. Why? Consider this, by Richard Allington:

The research on comprehension strategy instruction provides powerful evidence that most struggling readers (and many not so struggling readers) benefit enormously when we can construct lessons that help make the comprehension process visible. Many students only develop the strategies they need with much instructional support . . . these students need demonstrations of effective strategy use and lots of opportunities to apply the demonstrated strategy over time. (2005, 98)

I continue to read aloud, thinking aloud about my new learning and encouraging kids to share theirs. We learn, respond, and I record their comments on sticky notes.

- *Teeth*: They use up thousands of teeth in a lifetime and never run out. Some have twenty rows!
- *Skin*: Sandpapery with skin—teeth called denticles (Beware! Don't touch!)
- *Body Temperature*: Cold-blooded
- *Migration*: They migrate just like whales do!
- *Jaws and Teeth*: WOW! Some bite almost three hundred times harder than we do/can cut through steel
- *Kinds of Sharks*: Tiger, mako, great white, whale, basking, blue, nurse
- *Food*: marine mammals, other sharks, shellfish
- *Sharks Are Fish*: Like/teeth and backbone; unlike/no other bones; just cartilage/drawing of nose and ear

Now it's almost time for kids to have a go with a partner at reading, recognizing, talking about, and recording new learning. But before I send them off, I make my most important point.

"Boys and girls, before you begin working with your partners, let's take a look at our file and see if we can make some connections between new learning and what we already know. Hmmm . . .

"Oh! Look at this! See this sticky note here—the one that says, 'Shark skin is sandpapery and has skin-teeth called denticles'? And remember earlier, when we wrote, 'Sharks have rough skin'? Do you see the connection between the two? Before we read the book, we already knew that sharks have rough skin. But in our reading we learned that a shark's skin feels sandpapery and has skin-teeth called denticles, right? So we've confirmed that a shark's skin is rough—let's put a *C* for *confirmed* right on the sticky note like this—and we learned that shark skin has skin-teeth called denticles.

"So let's take this sticky note, the one that says, 'Shark skin is sandpapery . . .' out of New Learning and attach it to this one, the one that says, 'Sharks have rough skin' in the Our Schema—What We Think We Know section." (I physically take it out of New Learning and attach it to the bottom of the sticky note that says, "Sharks have rough skin.") "Do you see what we're doing? We're connecting new learning to what we already know—I'm thinking this is just how it works inside our brains!

"We already knew that a shark's skin is rough. Now we can add more specific information to our brainfiles—I think I'm always going to remember that a shark's skin feels sandpapery and that it has skin-teeth called denticles. And doesn't the word *denticles* remind you of the word *dentist*? That will help us remember, too. I can just see those little teeth so clearly in my mind. What about you?

"You, too? And Shyann, are you saying you can almost feel the shark's rough skin in your mind? That's amazing. You'd better be careful!

"Do you see any other connections we can make?" They do! Figure 5.4 in the color insert shows the way our file looks after we make connections to schema. It isn't common for all new learning to connect to what children already know, but this day it does.

When we send children off to work with their partners, we ask them to choose a book from one of the shark tubs at their tables, asking them to check two things:

1. that one or both of them can read the text easily
2. that there are opportunities for new learning through the pictures, text, or both

Once they've selected their books, we ask them to read a page or two together, stop and talk about what they just read, and focus their reading *and* their conversation in two ways.

1. *The content*: When you read, what are you learning about sharks that you didn't know before? Talk with each other first, and then record your new learning on a sticky note in pictures and/or words, telling what's important, in a way that makes sense to both of you, without telling too much.
2. *The process*: When you read, talk, and record new learning today, ask yourself, "What am I learning about myself as a reader today? What am I learning about myself today that I might try tomorrow and in the days and weeks to come?"

Once children get settled (see Figure 5.5), Valerie and I move about the room and confer with partners about their new learning, connections, and

FIGURE 5.5
"Wow! Did you hear that?
We'd better write that down!"

what they're noticing about themselves as readers, learners, and thinkers. After about thirty minutes, we ask children to take a look at their sticky notes and choose one or two to share. We ask them to put those sticky notes on the cover of their books. We explain that they'll be sharing their new learning about sharks *tomorrow*, and that now they're all set. We let them know that *today* during share time we'll be focusing on what they learned about themselves as readers. "Think about what you learned about yourselves today that will help you in the days to come," we say. Figures 5.6 and 5.7 in the color insert show the work students did on day two of our lesson.

Postscript

On day two Valerie and I walk her kids to PE after the share, and when we come back to the classroom, we find eight-year-old Roxie standing in front of the shark file, deep in concentration. She has a bright orange sticky note in her hand, and we watch as she moves it from the New Learning section of the file up to Our Schema—What We Think We Know section and then back down again.

FIGURE 5.8
The sticky note that goes with Roxie's thinking.

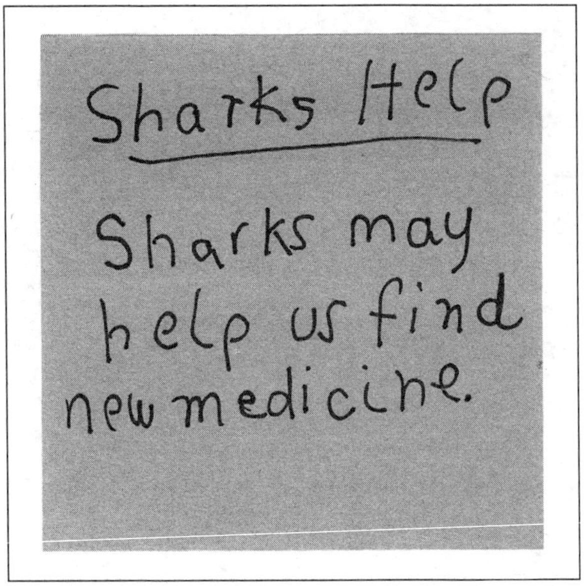

Sharks Help

Sharks may help us find new medicine.

"What's up, Roxie?" Valerie asks. "I bet your relay team is wondering where you are!"

"I know, but I'm trying to figure something out."

"What are you trying to figure out?"

"What do you do with new learning that doesn't connect to anything? Like this says, 'Sharks may help us find new medicine.' It doesn't, well, it doesn't really connect to anything up here," she says, pointing to the What We Think We Know part of the file. "So what are we supposed to do with it?" (see Figure 5.8).

Valerie and I look at each other, neither of us quite sure what to say. But she's the first to find just the right words.

"You're right, that is a big question, Roxie," Valerie says with a smile. "What do you think we should do?"

Roxie gives the question some thought and finally says, "Hmmm. Well, I think we should *definitely* take it out of New Learning, 'cause it's not really new anymore. We know it now. Maybe we should, um, just put it in Our Schema even if we don't have anything to connect it to? It can just hang out there until we do."

"Brilliant thinking, Roxie," I tell her. "You really worked hard to figure that out." And Roxie, Valerie, and I put our hands together in a three-way mighty-high-five!

CHAPTER 6

Lesson Design: Creating Lessons Based *on* Principles *and* Practices You Believe In

I believe the gradual release of responsibility instructional model, integrated into a workshop format, best guides children toward understanding and independence. (Pearson and Gallagher 1983)

■ ■ ■ ■ ■ ■ ■ Let's begin this chapter by reflecting a bit on the last one. In Chapter 5, we plunged into one lesson, getting a glimpse into what an interactive, engaging lesson with real-world applications looks and sounds like. As you were reading, what kinds of things did you notice? What did it make you think about? What do you wonder?

Sometimes when teachers read about or observe classrooms like this one, they say, "How does everything just seem to come together?" There's the tiniest hint of uncertainty in these words, like maybe it was just a lucky happenstance that things worked the way they did. I understand. I've asked that question, too.

But now I know things went the way they did that day not because of some lucky happenstance, but because Valerie and I were intentional in our teaching. We envisioned what we wanted for her kids and set about making our vision reality. We planned our work and worked our plan! To guide us, we used a lesson design tool I've developed over the years that incorporates the practices and principles I believe in (see Figure 6.1 and the blank form in the appendix).

In this chapter and the next one I take an in-depth look into this tool, explaining how it came to be and how it works for me. Just like the mental files lesson, the point isn't that it will fit your needs exactly, but that it will encourage you to develop your own lesson design tool (if you don't have one already) that reflects who you are and what you believe about teaching and learning.

Because student understanding and independence are central to my teaching, the gradual release of responsibility instructional model (Pearson and Gallagher 1983) informs my lesson design. Whether lessons are intended for readers, writers, mathematicians, or scientists; or the children I'm planning for, who are five, nine, or twelve years old; this instructional model, integrated into a workshop format, guides me as I plan.

FIGURE 6.1

Lesson Design

What is the focus of the lesson? What do I want students to learn?

Why is this important? How will it help students?

How do I use this skill or strategy myself?

What connections can I help students make?

The gradual release of responsibility model of instruction includes the following elements (adapted from Pearson and Gallagher 1983):

Teacher Modeling

- Teachers explain the focus of the lesson and why it's important.
- Teachers demonstrate how they use this skill or strategy.
- Teachers think aloud to make their thinking visible.

Guided Practice **Within** *the Lesson*

- Teachers engage students in focused discussions.
- Teachers and students practice together.
- Teachers scaffold students' attempts.
- Summation (What did we learn?) focuses on content and process.

Guided Practice **Beyond** *the Lesson*

- Teachers scaffold students' attempts as children work together to apply new learning in pairs and small groups.
- Teachers encourage and support student work and thinking, giving feedback that honors the child and the task.
- Students share their learning and thinking processes with each other.

Independent Practice

- Students work to apply and refine new learning independently.
- Students continue to receive regular feedback from their teacher and peers.

Application

- Students apply the new learning in authentic situations.
- Students transfer learning from one situation to another.
- Students synthesize content and process.

When I first became aware of the gradual release of responsibility model, creating a lesson design tool that incorporated its phases would have been out of the question. I may have understood it conceptually, but I wasn't anywhere near putting it into play. No wonder.

Back then I was used to marching through teacher's guides and textbooks from beginning to end, start to finish. Children and I flitted from one topic to another—it was like we studied everything and nothing. But this new way of thinking about teaching and learning was dramatically different. In this instructional model, independence and understanding were the intended outcomes and gradually releasing responsibility to students was the means to that end. Flitting was no longer fitting.

How did I move forward? Interested colleagues and I began by observing teachers who knew more about this model than we did. After these observations, we'd come back to school energized by what we'd seen. We couldn't stop thinking and talking about those teachers and their kids! Children in these classrooms *chose* their books, they *talked* to each other in sophisticated ways about their learning, and they *worked independently* for long periods of time. It seemed as if everyone was totally, joyfully engaged.

The teachers we observed thought aloud during read-alouds and throughout the day, conferred with children, and took notes about what they learned. They smiled. They looked happy. They were totally engaged, too! These teachers trusted themselves and they trusted children—there was shared responsibility for teaching and learning.

Could my kids do that? I'd wondered. And deep down inside I suspect I was mostly wondering, Could *I* do that? The teachers I'd observed made it appear so easy. I just couldn't figure out how they seemed to know what to say, what to do, and where to take their children next.

That was the hard part. How do I go about figuring out these things? I'd wondered. How do some teachers just seem to know?

I used to think maybe it was something intuitive—that there were these magical teachers out there who just naturally knew what to do. Were they just born that way? I remember wondering. Back then I had serious doubts I would ever become a teacher like that.

But now I know that magic has little to do with it. Now I know that learning where my kids need to go next begins with finding out where they are now. I find out where kids are by asking thoughtful questions and expecting thoughtful answers, listening more and talking less, and creating learning opportunities that engage students and make their learning and thinking visible. I reflect on what children say and do, consider the big picture, and think about where it makes sense to go next. And then I do it all over again. Once we have the end in mind, we set about putting the means into motion.

The Lesson Design Tool: An In-depth Look

Any time I'm teaching children something new, the gradual release of responsibility instructional model, integrated into a workshop format, directly informs my lesson design. Before, during, and after each lesson (for me, these are usually whole-group lessons, but the same would hold true for small-group work), I work hard in these ways:

- *I explain* to students the focus of the lesson and why it's important to make connections (when I can) to previous learning (this takes place during the time-to-teach part of the workshop, within the modeling phase of gradual release).
- *I show kids how* by modeling, thinking aloud, and demonstrating what I want them to learn how to do (this takes place during the time-to-teach part of the workshop, within the modeling phase of gradual release).
- I give children significant time to *practice* in a variety of authentic ways with an appropriate range of materials, offering feedback all the while (this takes place during the time-to-read-and-respond part of the workshop, within the guided and independent practice phases of gradual release).
- I provide time for students to *reflect, share, and teach* each other (this takes place during the time-to-reflect-share-and-teach part of the workshop, within the independent practice and application phases of gradual release).
- *I assess* where students are (this takes place throughout the workshop and all phases of gradual release).
- *I reflect* and *consider next steps* (this takes place after the workshop).

For another way to show integration of the gradual release of responsibility model and a workshop format, see Figure 6.2.

FIGURE 6.2 INTEGRATING THE GRADUAL RELEASE OF RESPONSIBILITY INSTRUCTIONAL MODEL INTO A WORKSHOP FORMAT

	Components of the Workshop			
	Time to Teach	**Time to Practice**	**Time to Reflect, Share, and Teach**	**Ongoing Assessment**
Phases of Gradual Release	15–20 minutes whole group	30–60 minutes small group, pairs, individually	10–15 minutes whole group, small groups, pairs	throughout the workshop throughout the phases of gradual release
Modeling, Thinking Aloud, Demonstration	✓	✓	✓	✓
Guided Practice	✓	✓	✓	✓
Independent Practice		✓	✓	✓
Application		✓	✓	✓

Explain the Lesson's Focus, Why It's Important, and More

Knowing what a lesson's focus is sounds pretty basic, right? But have you ever been in the middle of a lesson and wondered, What's my point here? Or, Why am I spending time on this? How is this moving children forward? Taking time to think through the focus of the lesson, identify why it's important to students (in school and in the real world), and make connections from this lesson to previous learning increases the lesson's relevance to students and the likelihood of success. And when we think about how we use the skill or strategy we're teaching and share these experiences with students before the lesson, we provide added clarity for ourselves and students. See Figure 6.3 for how I answered these questions before the sharks/mental file lesson.

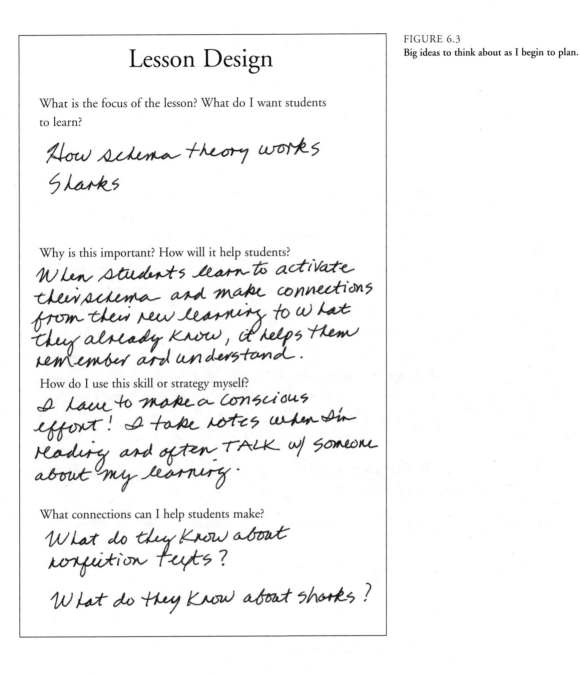

FIGURE 6.3
Big ideas to think about as I begin to plan.

Lesson Design

What is the focus of the lesson? What do I want students to learn?

How schema theory works
Sharks

Why is this important? How will it help students?

When students learn to activate their schema and make connections from their new learning to what they already know, it helps them remember and understand.

How do I use this skill or strategy myself?

I have to make a conscious effort! I take notes when I'm reading and often TALK w/ someone about my learning.

What connections can I help students make?

What do they know about nonfiction texts?

What do they know about sharks?

When we're thoughtful in our planning, we lend purpose, focus, and direction to our teaching. Likewise, when students are clear about what they're going to be learning, why it's important, and how it will help them, it gives purpose, focus, and direction to their learning, too. Here are some examples from the mental files/sharks lesson.

I'm being clear about what *it is we're going to be learning how to do* when I say this:

> *"Today and tomorrow we're going to work together to learn some specific things we can do to help us understand and remember new learning."*

I'm letting children know why *these lessons are going to be important to them—how this information will help them—in the classroom and the world*—when I say this:

> *"But here's a problem I have, and I'm wondering if this ever happens to you. Have you ever been reading a great nonfiction text that's full of important information? Maybe it's a magazine, a book, or one of your textbooks. Maybe it's even something you learned online or while watching The Discovery Channel. Then another day you're talking with a friend, or your mom or dad, or your teacher, and you want to tell them all about what you read or saw or heard, only you can't remember what you learned."*

And I'm helping students make connections to previous learning when I say this:

> *"When you read nonfiction, what are some of the things you can almost always count on? What are some things you already know about this type of text?"*

Showing Kids How

Thoughtful teachers everywhere know that the best way to begin teaching children something new is to *show them how*. Figure 6.4 shows my plan for the mental files/sharks lesson. Whether it's modeling reading behaviors, thinking aloud about our mental processes, or demonstrating how it looks and sounds to work with a partner, showing is always better than telling.

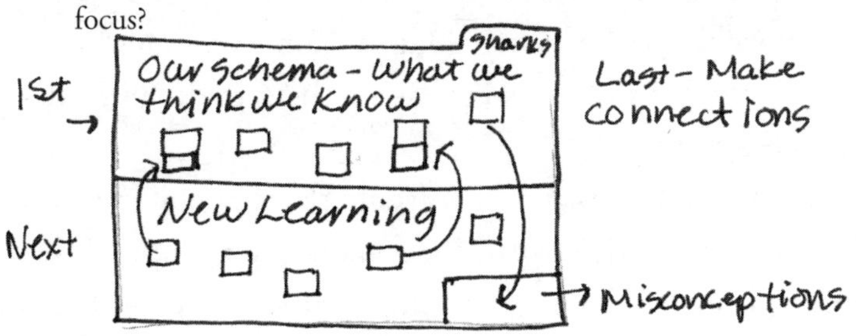

FIGURE 6.4
Thinking through whole-group work.

Showing Students How

Modeling/Thinking Aloud

■ What books and/or materials will I need?

★ Sharks by Seymour Simon – find 4 or 5 paragraphs to read aloud

★ Sticky notes, 3×3, 2 colors

★ Large file folder – make from poster board and laminate

Demonstration

■ Are there structures or formats that I need to show students how to do?

Do Valerie's kids know about turn and talk? Ask. If not – fish bowl it.

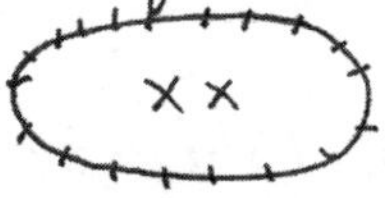

Guided Practice

■ How will I release responsibility to students during the lesson?

★ Invite students into the conversation

★ Turn and talk – " Put your new learning in your own words, in a way that makes sense, without telling too much."

■ Will students and I co-construct an anchor chart? What is its focus?

1st → Our schema – what we think we know · sharks
Next · New Learning
Last – Make connections
→ Misconceptions

We're showing students our dedication and passion for teaching and learning; we're sharing how we think, who we are, and the kinds of things we want for them. Here are some examples that concern our shark file and demonstrate these points.

I'm being explicit about* how *we're going to begin learning strategies for helping us remember and understand what we read and learn by making the process visible when I say this:

> *"Now, here's where we're going to record all the things we think we know about sharks—let's label this Our Schema—What We Think We Know."*

I'm demonstrating just what I want kids to do when they record their new learning on sticky notes when I say this:

> *"I'm going to write the word 'Gills' with a line under it for the heading of my sticky note, like this, and under it I'll write* five *to seven sets—I think I'll even draw them, like this."*

And I'm showing kids just how I think schema theory works when I say this:

> *"So let's take this sticky note, the one that says, 'Shark skin is sandpapery . . .' out of New Learning and attach it to this one, the one that says, 'Sharks have rough skin,' in the Our Schema—What We Think We Know section."*

It's a fine line I walk when thinking aloud. I want to be sure I model *enough*, so children know just what it is I'm asking them to do, but I don't want to go on and on either.

Over the years I've learned that I *need* feedback from children when I'm teaching. Do I need to slow down? Model more? Speed up? Move in another direction entirely? Without student feedback, I'd just plow through, start to stop, never really knowing. And that just doesn't seem like good practice.

I want students to have a go at trying out what I'm asking them to do early on. I want them to think, "Oh! I'm going to be able to do this." Inviting students to turn and talk with each other and participate in class discussions are two ways to imbed guided practice opportunities into lessons, giving students a chance to practice in a supportive context and me a chance to find out what they're thinking and where they are in the learning process.

So I love when Valerie's computer whiz, Raul, says, "Hey! That's just like deleting! You just push a button in your brain and poof! Away it goes!" When children join in the conversation and share their understandings, I feel like, "Okay. Now we're getting somewhere." Children's thoughtful voices bring life to my teaching, and joy to learning by offering ideas and perspectives that are different from my own.

Children's voices keep my teaching real. When they make my teaching their own—when they synthesize information like Raul did—they not only enhance everyone's understanding but also inspire other children to think for themselves. And by acknowledging thoughtful responses by saying, "Raul, I never thought about it that way, but that's just what it's like, and exactly what we want to do," I'm letting children know that I'm a teacher and a learner, and that they are teachers and learners, too.

I want the tone of my lessons to reflect what I believe about teaching and learning. I'm all about a conversational, we're-in-this-together, let's-see-what-we-can-figure-out kind of tone. I always hope the students I work with think about our time together as a joint venture—make that *adventure*—into teaching, learning, and discovery.

Anchor charting most often comes into play during this time, too. Whether I'm taking notes in my notebook to create one later or crafting one on the spot, anchor charts make children's thinking and learning visible and concrete. The mental file folder is one example of an anchor chart that serves children in these ways: it makes children's understanding and learning about sharks visible, and it highlights in a concrete way just how schema theory works.

And later, when children assume responsibility for using individual file folders in their independent reading, we can point to the shark file as a handy reference and reminder of how they can go about it on their own, with their individual, regular-sized file folders!

When deciding whether or not to include an anchor chart, I ask myself these questions:

■ What is its purpose?
■ In what ways will it be useful to students?
■ How will it support ongoing learning?

And when creating an anchor chart, I believe that these points are important, too:

- It focuses on one key idea.
- It is co-constructed with students.
- It is readable and clearly organized; that is, kids can read the words and understand the ideas.

Guided and Independent Practice

The next part of the workshop is for children to practice, in a variety of authentic ways, what we're teaching them. When I plan for this time, I think about the kinds of books and materials students will need, what they will do and the supports they'll need in order to be successful, and what I will do (see Figure 6.5).

What Books and/or Materials Will Students Need?

Intentional teachers spend significant time searching for just the right books for modeling reading behaviors, teaching specific skills, and thinking aloud as they read. We spend hours rummaging through our classrooms, schools, and public libraries, picking the brains of colleagues, reading reviews, searching online, and browsing about in bookstores. We take the time because we know the difference a perfect book can make.

And yet, when we send students off to practice the behaviors, skills, and strategies we are working so hard to teach them, we may not be as thoughtful about the kinds of books and materials *they* are reading. We sometimes assume that anything will do. Not so.

When we send children off to practice, we want to do all we can to ensure that they are practicing with books that maximize our teaching and their learning. Their books, just like ours, need to be worthy of what it is we're asking them to do. Valerie purposely gathered books she knew would interest and engage her students, and they made their choices from these selections. No matter which book or books children chose to read, she knew they would be successful at learning something new, whether it was from reading the words or looking carefully at the photographs, cutaways, diagrams, close-ups, and other nonfiction conventions.

Guided and Independent Practice

What books and/or materials will students need?

* tubs of shark books at tables
* sticky notes, 3×3, orange
* Sharpie pens

What do I want students to do?

■ individually _____

_____

■ and/or in (pairs) *read, talk, record new learning on sticky notes*

■ and/or in small groups _____

_____

What will I do?
✓ confer   ✓ observe
✓ listen in   ____ meet with students in small groups

Reflect, Share, Teach

Day 2

Guiding questions for students

■ What did you learn (content)? How will you teach us?
    about sharks

Day 1

■ What did you learn about yourself as a reader today that you didn't know before (process)? How will you teach us?

How was it working w/a partner today? What did you learn about yourselves? Was recording your new learning helpful? How?

What Do I Want Students to Do?

Depending on what students are learning and where they are in the process, I might ask them to work independently, in pairs, or in small groups. Or I might meet with a small group of children who have similar needs while some children work in pairs and still others independently. It's all about knowing students and individualizing instruction during this time.

Because I was asking Valerie's kids to do something new that day, working with partners was a good choice for releasing responsibility; most children weren't yet ready to read, think about their new learning, and record it independently. But doing all that with a partner? No problem!

And even if they had been ready to work individually, I probably would have given them the option of working with a partner. That's because I believe in the social nature of learning. I want kids to talk! I want them to share ideas, puzzle through something together, and listen and learn from each other. Partner work is yet another way to support, engage, and create a collaborative, cooperative spirit in our classrooms and our schools.

Valerie and I also planned for her children to record their new learning on sticky notes as they worked with their partners. Why? We wanted to give them practice recognizing new learning, recording it in their own words in a way that makes sense and without telling too much. We wanted evidence of how kids were applying what we'd taught them. And, we wanted students to bring their sticky notes back to the group and put them on the New Learning section of the mental file folder so we could see what kinds of connection children made between new learning and what they already knew. Who knew that a small stack of sticky notes could teach us so much!

When asking kids to respond, I want to make certain that the ways I ask them to make their thinking visible are meaningful. To ensure this, I ask myself these questions:

- Is what I'm asking kids to do purposeful and authentic?
- Does it make student thinking visible?
- Is this way of responding open-ended, allowing for a wide range of responses?
- Will it engage students?
- Do children have opportunities over time to respond in a variety of oral, written, and artistic ways?
- Does this way of responding serve as a means to comprehension and understanding (for the child) as well as a measure (for the teacher)?

What Will I Do?

What's the teacher doing while children are practicing? Conferring with pairs and individuals, listening in on conversations, meeting with children in small groups as needed, and standing back to observe the big picture are the things I consistently do. Taking action in these ways gives me clear direction for tomorrow's lessons.

Valerie and I sat at tables and on the floor, conferring with students, listening in, asking questions, and recording what we learned. On this day, we resisted the temptation to tell, to push our ideas on children or give them advice. I'd already shown them enough to get them started, and now we were assessing and learning how students were making sense of things; they were having a go with the support of each other. Later, we could compare notes, reflect, and think about next steps based on what we'd learned.

Reflect, Share, Teach

At the end of guided and independent practice time, I always bring children back together in the meeting area so they/we can reflect on what they learned about themselves as readers (or writers or mathematicians or scientists) that day, share what they've learned, and teach others. I include this time, as well as some guiding questions for students, in the lesson design tool (see Figure 6.6). Children have opportunities for sharing content, but I also ask students to think about questions like these:

- What did I learn about myself as a learner today that I can use in the days and weeks to come?
- What do I understand about myself as a reader now that I didn't understand before?
- How can I teach others what I've learned?

Why? I want students to understand *how* they go about constructing meaning. I model how I do it, but in the end they'll need to figure out how it works for them. Having daily opportunities to teach each other what they've learned *and* how they've gone about learning it sends a strong message. We're saying, "I will show you how I go about doing this, but in the end, I want you to figure out how this works for you." They're developing the tools they need to be successful and the confidence they need to push through when they encounter difficulty.

Guided and Independent Practice

What books and/or materials will students need?

* *tubs of shark books at tables*
* *sticky notes, 3×3, orange*
* *Sharpie pens*

What do I want students to do?

■ individually _____

■ and/or in (pairs) *read, talk, record new learning on sticky notes*

■ and/or in small groups _____

What will I do?

✓ confer   ✓ observe

✓ listen in   _____ meet with students in small groups

Reflect, Share, Teach

Day 2

Guiding questions for students

■ What did you learn (content)? How will you teach us?
  \ *about sharks*

Day 1

■ What did you learn about yourself as a reader today that you didn't know before (process)? How will you teach us?

How was it working w/a partner today? What did you learn about yourselves? Was recording your new learning helpful? How?

FIGURE 6.6
Thinking through ways to help students reflect on themselves as learners, share, and teach others.

Final Thoughts

What if, despite your best efforts and hard work, the lesson you've designed doesn't work? What if kids just don't get it? It's not the end of the world, and it happens to everyone. Don't give up! Find a quiet moment to regroup and rethink. Did you assume too much? Do you need to model more?

Would a different book help? Figure out what you need to do tomorrow that you didn't do today. Own it, and move on.

When this happens to me, I say something like this to students: "Boys and girls, remember our lesson yesterday? I did some thinking last night in my notebook—see all my writing? And I realized that there were some things I forgot to show you how to do. No wonder we were frustrated! Are you willing to have a go again today? Thank you. I can't wait to share with you my new thinking, and I'd love to hear from you, too. Are you ready?"

It's a wonderful message we send to children when we use this kind of language. We're showing them that as their teacher, we don't always get things right the first time, we'll do everything we can to teach them well, and we don't give up on ourselves *or* the children we teach. Just as we want our kids to see themselves as the kind of kids who can figure things out, we need to see ourselves that way, too. Is the sense of agency alive and well within you?

CHAPTER 7

Assessment, Reflections, *and* Next Steps

I believe formative, ongoing assessment enlightens and informs my day-to-day work with children.

■ ■ ■ ■ ■ ■

We hear a lot about assessment nowadays—we teachers don't seem to get very far into a conversation without this topic coming into play. We talk about summative assessments—the kind that occur *after* instruction (when all is said and done)—and formative, authentic assessments—the kind that are ongoing and show us how children have progressed over time.

Summative assessments are seen as a way to measure, at a particular point in time, student learning as it relates to content standards. Though the information gleaned from this type of assessment can be important, it's too late in the learning process to make adjustments to our teaching. Stephanie Harvey likens summative assessment to an autopsy—examiners try to determine why the patient died, what the contributing factors might have been, and implications (perhaps) for future patients. But it's too bad, so sad, for this particular patient.

But formative assessments are different. They allow us to make adjustments in our work with children *before* an autopsy is required! Consider this statement by Erma Bombeck:

> *I see our children as kites. You spend a lifetime trying to get them off the ground. You run with them until you're both breathless . . . they crash . . . you add a longer tail . . . they hit the rooftop . . . you pluck them out of the spouting . . . you patch and comfort, adjust and teach. You watch them lifted by the wind and assure them that someday they'll fly. . . . Finally, they are airborne, but they need more string and you keep letting it out. With each twist of the ball of twine, there is a sadness that goes with the joy because the kite becomes more distant and somehow you know it won't be long before this beautiful creature will snap the lifeline binding you together and soar as it was meant to soar—free and alone.* (1971, 165)

When we ask students to make their thinking visible during the process of learning something new, these authentic responses are the kinds of formative assessments that guide our instruction. For example, when Valerie's students recorded their new learning on sticky notes, she then had valuable information concerning where they were in the process. We don't attach grades to this kind of work; instead, we consider the implications for next steps. The time for grading comes at the end of the teaching and learning process, not during it.

Consider this analogy by Catherine Garrison and Michael Ehringhaus:

What if, before getting your driver's license, you received a grade every time you sat behind the wheel to practice driving? What if your final grade for the driving test was the average of all of the grades you received while practicing? Because of the initial low grades you received during the process of learning to drive, your final grade would not accurately reflect your ability to drive a car. In the beginning of learning to drive, how confident or motivated to learn would you feel? Would any of the grades you received provide you with guidance on what you needed to do next to improve your driving skills? Your final driving test, or summative assessment, would be the accountability measure that establishes whether or not you have the driving skills necessary for a driver's license—not a reflection of all the driving practice that leads to it. (Garrison and Ehringhaus)

Formative ways of assessing where children are in the learning process include

- *Conferring.* When we pull up a chair and sit next to a child to talk with them about their learning, we learn valuable information about how individual children are processing what we've taught them. And when we look at our conferences as a whole, we can use this information to consider the implications for small, needs-based groups and whole-group instruction.
- *Listening in.* Listening to what students say and recording what's pertinent in our notebooks, whether during whole-class discussions, short turn-and-talk sessions, or spontaneous conversations, yields us important, in-the-moment information. And writing it down helps us remember it!
- *Observing.* What do you notice? Ask yourself questions like, What's the overall level of engagement? What are kids really doing? Are there children who appear to be in need of more support? Less support?
- *Examining student work samples.* Looking carefully at student work samples and artifacts for evidence of understanding.

- *Charting student thinking.* When we capture student learning and thinking on anchor charts, we make it visible, public, and permanent, giving us insight into where students are in the process.
- *Reflecting, sharing, and teaching.* Taking notes when students reflect, share, and teach is one of the most significant ways to gauge student understanding.

Once we have all this information, what do we do with it? How do we use it to inform our instruction? We take time to study it! When Valerie and I sat down together after school to reflect on the lesson and to plan possible next steps, we gathered our notebooks, notes from student conferences, and the sticky-note-studded shark books kids were reading to guide us as we planned for the days ahead. What did we learn? Plenty! Here are some examples.

We learned from conferences I scripted between Valerie and her kids

This is from Daniel, after Valerie asked him what he'd learned about himself as a reader today.

> *"Well, um, I never knew Raul and I could work so great together. We can't sit by each other on the rug because we talk too much, but we're really good partners! Right, Raul?"*

This is from Roseanna and Riley, after Valerie asked them about their understanding of the mental file.

Roseanna: Well I think it's kinda sorta like we have all these things we've learned floating around in our heads. And we have to attach it to something or it just keeps on floating and floating and floating around forever.

Riley: Yeah. Like you have to lasso it (*swinging hand in a circling motion above her head*) and pull it in and put it right where it belongs!

Roseanna: Oh! Now I've got it! You lasso all the stuff you learned that's floating around in your head and then you put it in your files!

FIGURES 7.1A, B
Mara and Sondu's sticky notes
with added page numbers.

Riley: Just like at home. Pants in the pants drawer. Shirts in the shirt
    drawer. Socks in the sock drawer.
Roseanna: And UNDERWEAR in the UNDERWEAR drawer!

(You can't believe the hilarity this last comment generated. But then again,
maybe you can!)

And this from Mara and Sondu, when asked about the numbers they'd
written on their sticky notes (see Figure 7.1a, b).

Mara: Those are page numbers.
Sondu: Like here, where we wrote, "tail fin = caudal fin." That's on
    page 21 so that's why we have a 21 here. So we can find it
    again or something.
Mara: I have a good idea! We should write the title of the book, too,
    right by the 21! Then we can really find it!

(As we leave them, Mara's writing *Hunting Sharks* right before the num-
ber 21 and Sondu is doing the same with another sticky note that reads,
"Sharks swim and hunt when they are brand new babies! HONIST!!!
Page 25.")

We learned from listening in

The children had so many questions! They were asking each other and writing down things like this:

- Why do sharks have so many sets of gills?
- What are dorsal fins?
- Do shark pups come from shark eggs?
- Why do most baby sharks die? (THAT IS SAD)
- Are sharks mammals?
- Why aren't sharks as smart as dolphins?
- Can something be a predator and prey?
- Can they breathe through the pores in their skin?
- Why are some sharks mean and some sharks nice?

We learned from observation

- Some children were so focused on reading and writing that they didn't do enough talking, and others were so focused on talking (albeit about sharks) that they didn't do enough reading and writing.
- Some partnerships worked better than others!
- Children needed a central place to store sticky notes so they didn't always have to ask Valerie for more.
- Some kids thought they were "done" when they really weren't.

We learned from children's sticky notes in general

- Some children were doing well at recording their new learning, but many were copying information directly from the text and others were writing just a word or two, and were unable to remember what it was about.
- Some children used headings, but many didn't.
- Sometimes what children wrote was inaccurate.

We learned from the reflect, share, and teach time

- Raul and Daniel; Roseanna and Riley; and Mara and Sondu shared what they'd learned about themselves as readers.

Reflections and Next Steps

Once Valerie and I looked closely at all the information we'd gathered, we considered next steps. To see what Valerie's next steps included, see the Reflections and Next Steps section of the Lesson Design Form (Figure 7.2).

You might be wondering if it's necessary to use the lesson design tool for every lesson you teach. You could, but you probably won't need to. I

FIGURE 7.2
Big ideas to think about after the lesson.

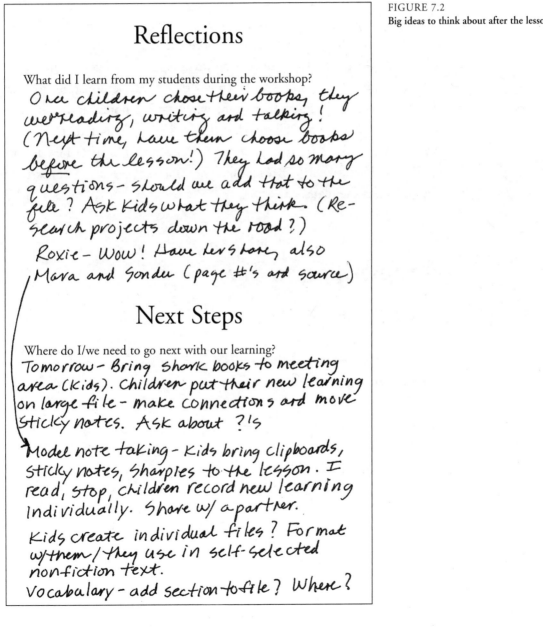

Reflections

What did I learn from my students during the workshop?

Once children chose their books, they were reading, writing and talking! (Next time, have them choose books before the lesson!) They had so many questions - should we add that to the file? Ask kids what they think. (Research projects down the road?)

Roxie - Wow! Have her share, also Mara and Sonder (page #'s and source)

Next Steps

Where do I/we need to go next with our learning?

Tomorrow - Bring shark books to meeting area (kids). Children put their new learning on large file - make connections and move sticky notes. Ask about ?'s

Model note taking - kids bring clipboards, sticky notes, sharpies to the lesson. I read, stop, children record new learning individually. Share w/ a partner.

Kids create individual files? Format w/ them / they use in self-selected nonfiction text.

Vocabulary - add section to file? Where?

usually began the week with one, but subsequent lessons (next steps) unfolded naturally based on what I'd learned from students. That's why the Reflections and Next Step lessons from the lesson design tool are so important. Information I learned from kids during discussions, small groups, and conferences directly informed the next-step lessons. These next-step lessons were structured the same, with time allocated for modeling, thinking aloud and/or demonstration, guided and independent practice, and reflection, sharing, and teaching. The content of these lessons reflects students' immediate needs as they relate to the initial lesson.

For example, one thing Valerie learned from the mental files lesson was that most of her children needed more explicit teaching on note taking. This might be the focus of several next-step lessons later in the week. When the time comes, she already knows that she'll demonstrate for her students what she considers important when taking notes, and then give them time to practice and share what they've learned about themselves as note takers that day. She doesn't necessarily need to fill out a new lesson design tool. Then, when her teaching focus changes, she can go back to it to guide her as she plans.

☑ Something to Try

Have you given some thought to developing a lesson design tool of your own? If you haven't but would like to, or if you're wondering where you might begin, you could start by using mine. Try it out for a couple of weeks. Then ask yourself:

- What seems to be working?
- What doesn't work?
- What might I add?
- What could I take away?

Rework it so that it fits you. Once you have something you like, I'm betting that you'll wonder how you ever got along without it!

CHAPTER 8

The Thoughtful Use *of* Time

I believe that a workshop format based on the elements of time, choice, response, and community fosters active, responsive teaching and learning. (Hansen 1987)

Sometimes when I talk with teachers about creating "the luscious feeling of endless time," they look at me like I've lost my mind. They tell me they love the *idea*, but with all they have to teach and all their kids need to learn, "There's no way," they say. "Luscious feeling? Endless time? Come on, girlfriend, get real!"

It's true that teachers have never been under more pressure. We're bombarded by demands and directives deemed by others as necessary and nonnegotiable. As a result, teachers everywhere are making Herculean efforts to fit everything in. It's no wonder there's talk by some of hurry-up-and-get-it-done.

But when getting done takes precedence over doing, when finishing becomes more important than figuring out, we've lost sight of why we became teachers in the first place; we've lost sight of what we know to be true. In our rush to try to fit everything in, we've forgotten that children learn by doing. And learning by doing takes time.

When kids are given time to puzzle through something that's challenging (with just enough support from their teachers to be successful) they're not only learning about the task at hand, they're learning about who they are and how they go about figuring things out. They're developing those can-do, let-me-have-at-it attitudes that we want so much for them.

It's hard to teach (and learn) with a timer in your head or one in your hand. It's controlling. It's restrictive. It limits mindfulness, understanding, and engagement for students and teachers alike. Just like reading fast isn't always about reading well, teaching fast isn't always about teaching well either. In Ellin Keene's remarkable book *To Understand* (2008) she reasons, "If we return to the conclusion that we learn most effectively when we learn *a few important concepts* at a time, taught *in depth over a long period*, and apply them in a *variety of texts and contexts*, then it becomes clear that we must be very clear about these concepts" (110).

No matter how fast we teach or how hard we try, it's impossible to do all we're being asked to do when teaching for understanding is our goal. So in the end . . .

Do we race through the day in a frantic sort of way, or do we slow down, determine what's essential, and teach those things deeply and well? Do we talk and tell and talk and tell and talk and tell some more, or do we show kids how and then give them lots of opportunities across the day for sharing in the responsibility for their learning?

It's difficult to confer deeply, listen carefully, and observe students closely when we're busily explaining the next newfangled way we're lining up, the hot-off-the-press test-prep packet, or the snazzy new center or station. When we have predictable structures and everyday routines in place, we don't need to spend precious time each day explaining what's to come. Kids already know.

And we also won't need to spend countless hours before and after school gathering materials, running off worksheets and packets, and doing whatever else we need to do to keep things up and running. Instead, we can think about where we know our kids have been, where we've learned they are now, and where we believe it makes the most sense to go next. Let's nix the juggling act and think about creating structures and routines that set the stage for thoughtful teaching and learning.

It takes courage to do the right thing. We have to learn to still those voices within us that say things like this:

> *"Come on! Don't tell me you're going to ask them to turn and talk with each other about their understanding of the last paragraph. You're already two chapters behind. You'll never get through this if you keep this up, so get a move on."*

And we need to listen to those other voices inside our heads that say (at the same time) . . .

> *"So what if I finish the textbook if kids don't understand the key concepts? Am I about covering and getting through, or am I more about uncovering content with kids and giving them the time and tools to understand big ideas deeply and well?"*

At some point we reach a fork in the road. Will we give children at least thirty minutes in the primary grades and forty-five minutes or more in the intermediate grades to read every day? Will we choose to confer with children when they read, or let them be? Will we build in time for students to reflect, share, and teach? When we consciously and consistently choose to listen to the voice that serves children best, that other voice becomes more and more distant and less and less insistent, and we begin to wonder why we ever gave it the time of day.

Think about this, by Lucy Calkins:

It is significant to realize that the most creative environments in our society are not the ever changing ones. The artist's studio, the researcher's laboratory, the scholar's library are deliberately kept simple so as to support the complexities of the work in progress. They are deliberately kept predictable so that the unpredictable can happen. (1983, 32)

Keep it simple. Those three words say it all when it comes to establishing creative classroom environments that support the complexities of teaching and learning. Putting into place a simple structure and a few well-thought-out routines encourages, nurtures, and allows teachers and learners significant time to commit to thoughtful teaching and learning, engage fully, and thrive.

When I think about the "unpredictable" happening, I think about two little boys named Torin and Colin. They were in my first-grade class, and we had been working on determining importance in fiction. I'd shown them how to go about navigating a traditional story map—kids were learning that identifying a story's setting, characters, problem, and the events that lead to solving the problem can help readers figure out the big ideas in a story.

One day I asked everyone, "So what are you thinking about story mapping? What do you understand after using a story map that you didn't understand before?" Kids said things like, "When I'm thinking all those things, I slow down and so I understand the story more" or, "When I get to know the characters, I can predict what they will say and do." But it was Torin's response that took me by surprise.

"It really doesn't help me at all," he said, "not even one little bit." He put his index finger parallel and very close to his thumb to further his point.

"Why not?" I asked.

"Well, we know more about stories than characters and problems and solutions," said Torin.

"Like what?"

"I'm not, um, really sure, but can Colin and I go work on it?"

Work on it they did, and twenty minutes later they came back with a two-page story map that was a definite improvement over the one I had given them!

FIGURE 8.1A
Torin and Colin's new and improved story map!

When I asked them if they'd teach everyone how to use it the next day, Torin looked at me, tilted his head to one side, and said, "Uh, Mrs. Miller. Don't you think we should try it out first, before we teach it?"

"Well, yes, absolutely," I responded, wondering why I hadn't said those same words myself. For a look at their original thinking, and how the three of us worked together to make it a bit easier for students to navigate, see Figure 8.1a and b.

Reading Workshop

Reading workshop is the best keep-it-simple structure I know. Typically sixty to ninety minutes in length, there is time every day for

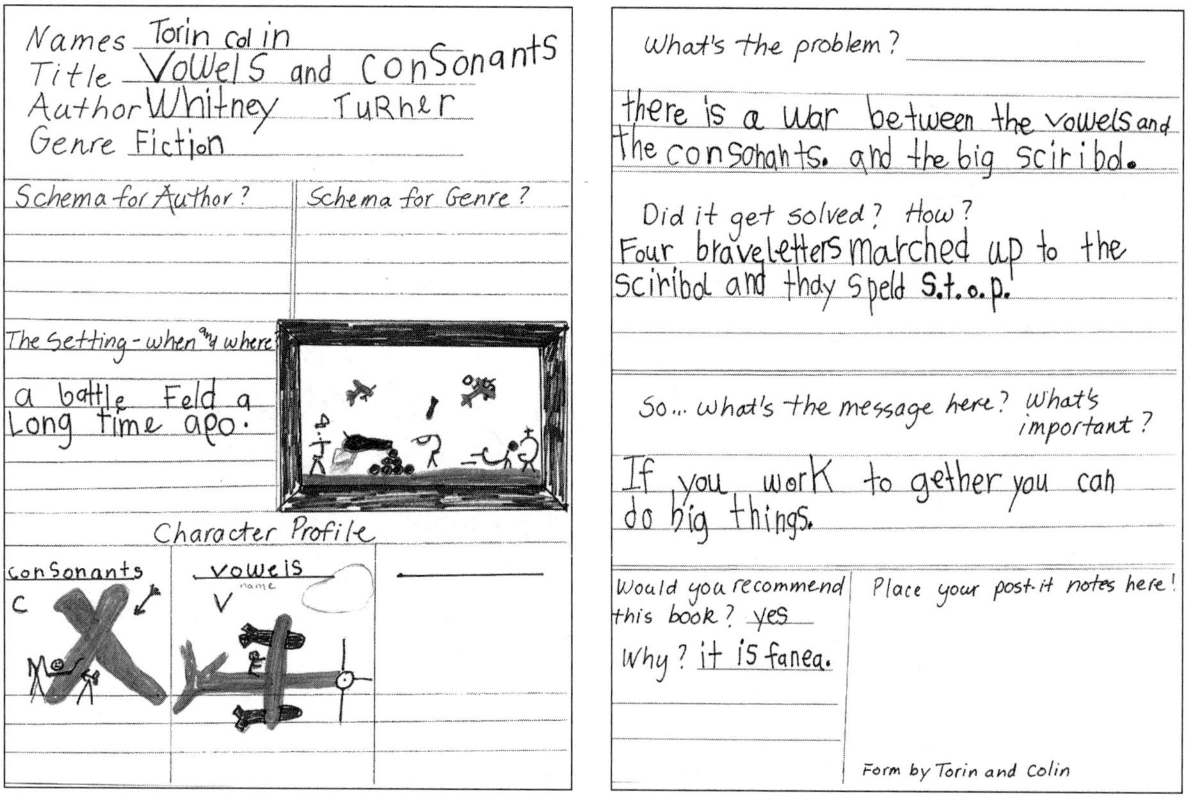

Names Torin colin
Title Vowels and Consonants
Author Whitney Turner
Genre Fiction

Schema for Author? | Schema for Genre?

The Setting - when *ny* where?
a battle Feld a
Long time ago.

Character Profile

consonants   vowels
    name
C   V

What's the problem? _____

there is a war between the vowels and
the consohants. and the big sciribd.

Did it get solved? How?
Four brave letters marched up to the
sciribd and thdy speld s.t.o.p.

So... what's the message here? What's
                              important?

If you work together you can
do big things.

Would you recommend | Place your post-it notes here!
this book? yes
Why? it is fanea.

Form by Torin and Colin

FIGURE 8.1B
Our adaptation of Colin and
Torin's original story map.

- teachers to teach through modeling, thinking aloud and/or demonstration (around fifteen minutes);
- students to read self-selected text, confer with their teacher and each other, and respond in a variety of authentic ways (thirty to forty-five minutes or more);
- students to reflect, share, and teach each other what they've learned about their reading and themselves as readers that day (around ten to fifteen minutes).

In my work in schools, it seems that most teachers are comfortable thinking aloud with students. Children have opportunities to choose at least some of the books they read, and most often there's at least some time set aside for independent reading. But when it comes to conferring, this one workshop essential seems to be missing in action.

Why? I'm not sure, because it's the best way I know to get to know kids as individual readers, writers, mathematicians, and scientists. When I confer with children, I learn how they're applying what I've taught them, where they need to go next. I'm building relationships, one child at a time. As Marie Clay says,

> *It is only when we know our children well and listen closely to their use of language that we can get inside the child's frame of reference and support the child's next forward moves. We must spend time* talking *with children, not* at *them.* (1998, 10)

Making the Case for Conferring

I'm working in the Teaching and Learning Center at Shadow Forest Elementary in Grand Rapids, Michigan, where Valerie Livingston's and Colleen Buddy's inviting classroom is home to teachers and students alike. I've just taught a lesson on synthesizing in fiction, and just before sending kids off to read and practice synthesizing self-selected picture books, I say, "Everyone, when you're reading independently or with a partner today, I'd like for you to pay attention to the process of synthesizing. Ask yourself these questions":

- How do I synthesize?
- How does this strategy work with other strategies I know about and use?
- What do I understand *after* synthesizing the story that I didn't understand before?

I wrap up with this:

> *I know these are big questions, but I'll be conferring—having a conversation—with some of you about these very things, and then in about forty minutes or so we'll all come back together and have a bigger conversation about what we learned about ourselves as readers and synthesizers today. Any thoughts? Questions? Okay. I can't wait to see what we find out. Good luck and Happy Reading!*

"Can you pleeease come here?" eleven-year-old Emelio mouths to me from across the room. I nod, make my way over to the little boy across the way, and sit on the floor beside him.

"What's up?" I whisper.

"Well, um, do I *really* have to read a picture book?"

"I thought we talked about this already, Emelio," I answer, "and didn't we all agree it was a smart idea?"

"Yeah, I know. But I'm, um, I'm really into poetry right now."

"I see. So you don't want to put your poetry books away and read something else for even a couple of days?"

"No."

"Hmmm. Well, what about this? You know how we've been working on synthesizing information in fiction? What would you think about doing some research on how readers go about synthesizing poetry?" Emelio nods.

"You think, maybe? That's great! Go get the poetry book you're reading and let's see what we can figure out."

He races over to the coat rack and pulls a well-worn sticky-noted copy of *Where the Sidewalk Ends* by Shel Silverstein from the depths of his backpack. "Listen to this one," he says as he sits back down beside me and opens the book to the page marked with a bright-green sticky note, five stars, and a small drawing of a snake with a very large bulge in its middle. "'Oh, I'm being eaten by a boa constrictor, a boa constrictor, a boa constrictor, I'm being eaten by a boa constrictor and I don't like it one bit. Well, what do you know? It's nibblin' my toe . . .'"

His eyes sparkle as he reads about (and becomes) a rather flamboyant boa constrictor. "Wow, Emelio," I say as he finishes. "That's the best rendition of 'Boa Constrictor' I've ever heard! I see on the chart over there you have Poetry Performances on Fridays—you should definitely sign up. And I can see why you love this book so much. I like it a lot, too.

"But let's think about our work today. When you were reading the poem, what were you thinking?"

"Well, um, I was just thinking it's really, really funny."

"So are you saying you're thinking the poem is funny, but there's not much else to think about?"

"Yeah."

"I see what you mean, and you know what? I'm thinking you might need a different *kind* of poem for our work today. Maybe you need one that is more challenging and focuses on big ideas. What do you think?"

"Mmmhmm. Kind of like that book we read—the one about the librarian."

"Exactly. I love Shel Silverstein, too, but I agree with you—he isn't going to work so well for us today, is he? Let's go look through the poetry tub and see what we can find."

We search through the red plastic tub marked Poetry, taking a look at *The Place My Words Are Looking For*, *Thirteen Moons on Turtle's Back*, *Poetry for Young People*, and *Words with Wings*.

He's overwhelmed. "Well, let's see," I say, paging slowly through the text. "What about this one, *Words with Wings*? I'm thinking this book of poetry might be perfect for you. What do you think?"

I take his slight nod as a yes. "I love how you're giving this a try, Emelio. So how about if you take some time to look through the book, read some of the poems, and find one you want to work with. *Next*, think about what we learned about synthesizing when we read *The Librarian of Basra*. Do you remember?"

"Well, I know I need to think about my thinking when I'm reading, and, well, maybe I'll change my mind? Like I'll be thinking the poem's about one thing, and then, um, a little later maybe I'll be thinking it's about something else?"

"You've got it. Understanding that your thinking may change, or evolve, as you're reading is a great way to begin to think about synthesizing.

"So now . . . once you've found your poem, how will you begin? What's your plan?"

"Read it?"

"Okay. Then what?"

"Stop and think what it's about? And then maybe read it again?"

"So you're saying you're going to read it all the way through, then stop and think what it's about? Then you're going to read it again and see if your thinking changes?"

"Yeah. *The Librarian of Basra* is long, so we had to stop a lot, but poems are short, so, um, I don't think I need to stop. I'm going to read it all the way to the end."

"That sounds like a great plan, Emelio. Try it and see what happens. I'll be back in a little while to see how it's working . . . I can't wait to see what we're going to learn about synthesizing poetry from you. Good luck!"

Right about now you might be wondering, "How do you justify spending so much time with one child? What about the twenty-four others who need your time and attention, too?"

It's true. In the time I spent conferring with Emelio, I could have easily touched base with three, four, five, maybe even six more children. But *touching base* isn't teaching. Touching base with children is a quick hi and 'bye with a little something in between.

Touching base is a good thing. That "little something in between" might be encouraging a child to keep at it, reminding a child to get back on track, or asking a child if she remembers what she learned in our conference yesterday to help her with her work today. Touching base is all about responding at the surface level to student behaviors. But don't confuse touching base with conferring.

Conferring is something else entirely. When we confer with students, we're not standing above them or even leaning over, we're sitting right beside them, shoulder to shoulder. We're digging deeper now, working hard to individualize our instruction and support children as they apply what we've taught them in large- and small-group settings.

Richard Allington said that his research indicates that our most effective teaching occurs when we work with students one-on-one. I've learned from him, others, and my own experience that it's not about how many children we confer with in a day, but how deeply we teach and touch those we do.

Think about Emelio. A quick "hi and 'bye" would not have sufficed this day. When I learn he doesn't want to read a picture book and he's "really into poetry" I have to make a decision. Will I force the issue, or will I listen to his plea?

I know that choice is important for readers of all ages, and so I choose to listen. And because I do, when we talk about choosing a different kind of poem, or I ask him to do some research on how readers go about synthesizing poetry, he listens to me. I've negotiated with Emelio on the type of text he'll read, but I haven't compromised the lesson or my teaching. When we work *with* children, they're more likely to work with us.

You might be thinking, "Okay. But did you really need to listen to him read 'Boa Constrictor'?" For me, the answer is yes. Emelio was sharing with me part of who he is, and it allowed me to acknowledge and revel in that for just a moment. I want to build relationships with the children in my charge; I teach and learn best when I know the children I'm teaching well. And besides, don't we all need a little Shel Silverstein in our lives now and then?

And what about the rest of the kids? Their day will come. Do you know the picture book *The Three Questions* by Jon Muth (2002)? It's a story about a little boy named Nickolai who is seeking the answers to three questions. He wonders:

When is the best time to do things?
Who is the most important one?
What is the right thing to do?

It's Leo, the wise old turtle, who helps Nickolai understand that the answers were inside him all along by saying,

Remember then that there is only one important time, and that time is now. The most important one is always the one you are with. And the most important thing is to do good for the one who is standing at your side. For these, my dear boy, are the answers to what is most important in this world. This is why we are here. (Muth 2002)

I spend time with Emelio because I want to "do good" for him. I know there are twenty-four others, and his teacher will do the same for each of them time and again in the days, weeks, and months to come. I can't reach everyone all in one day, but I can reach one or two or maybe even three. I reach, touch, and teach by being present, putting myself in the moment and focusing my full attention on the one sitting by my side.

And now for the rest of the story. When I stop back by to see how Emelio's doing, I find him hunched over the poem "Your World," by Georgia Douglas Johnson.

"So—how's it going?" I ask him. "How's your plan working?"

"Well, I can read the words and I've read it two times, but, um, I'm not really sure what it's about. It's kind of challenging."

"But it is just the kind of poem you were looking for, right? A challenging one with big ideas?"

He looks at me now like he's not so sure about that, and I realize this exchange is going to be more than a quick "hi and 'bye." He needs more support from me in order to be successful; we're back into conference mode! And so I say, "Let's read it together and see what we can figure out." We read softly:

Your World
by Georgia Douglas Johnson

Your world is as big as you make it.
I know, for I used to abide
in the narrowest nest in a corner.
My wings pressing close to my side.

But I sighted the distant horizon
Where the sky line encircled the sea
And I throbbed with a burning desire
to travel this immensity.

I battered the cordon around me
And cradled my wings on the breeze
Then soared to the uttermost reaches
With rapture, with power, with ease! (Johnson 2001)

"Hmmm," I say when we finish. "I see what you mean. This *is* challenging. Right now, Emelio, just off the top of your head, what are you thinking this poem is about?"

"Farmland?"

"Anything else?"

"Not really."

"So right now you're thinking the poem is about farmland, right? Remember when we read *The Librarian of Basra*, and in the beginning we thought it was going to be about this great library where everyone came to discuss 'matters of the world and matters of the spirit'? And then when we read that the 'books are more precious to her than mountains of gold' and she and her friends and neighbors took matters into their own hands and risked their lives to save them, we changed our minds, remember?

"And your original plan was to read the poem all the way through and stop and think what it's about, and then read it and stop and think again, right?

"So how about this? Let's try to make your thinking a little more visible. Let's take a piece of paper and divide it into thirds, like this. At the top of the first column, let's write 'My thinking now,' in the next column 'and now,' and in the third column, 'and now' again. You can write 'farmland' here, in the first one. That's perfect.

"Next, read it again and record what you're thinking here, and then read it again and do the same here. This is pretty much like your original plan, only now you're going to be recording your thinking."

"So you mean, um, you mean I have to read it two *more* times?" he asks.

"Well, you don't HAVE to, but I'm thinking that if you did, you might learn something about yourself as a reader of poetry today. You'll be doing some research here that will be important not only for you, but for the whole class. Are you up for it?"

His slight nod is all I need to continue. "Aaah, Emelio, I just *knew* you would be! Are you all set? Okay—this is going to be good. Don't feel like you have to rush; I know that thinking takes time. And I can't wait to see what you find out!" (To see what Emelio found out, see Figure 8.2.)

Synthesizing Poetry		
My thinking now...	and now...	and now.
I'm thinking about farm land.	I'm thinking about angels.	I'm thinking about a bird. At first I thought about farm land then I thought about angels. After synthesizing I'm thinking that the bird is in a nest at one point, then the bird kind of says "I need to explore the world because there is more to see. Emelio

FIGURE 8.2
Emelio's synthesis of "Your World" by Georgia Douglas Johnson.

Whew! That was hard work (for both of us). But isn't it the best kind of work? And isn't it this that keeps us coming back day after day after day?

When I stopped back by to see how Emelio was doing, he was struggling. He had no idea what the poem "Your World" was about, and frankly, I wasn't so sure either. When I think about what I'd have said early in my teaching career, it probably would have gone something like this: "You know what, Emelio? You're right. This really *is* challenging. Let's put this book away for now and find something else that's a little easier, okay?" In reality, it wouldn't have been so much about putting the book away for Emelio as it was putting the book away for me. Back then I suspect I wouldn't have trusted either one of us to try to figure out "Your World."

But when I find myself in situations like these nowadays, I remain calm, make a conscious effort to put myself in the moment, and ask myself my own three questions:

- What do I know about this child?
- What do I know about myself as a reader?
- What do I know about teaching kids to read?

In Emelio's case, my inner conversation sounded something like this.

What do I know about this child?

I know that he's willing to take risks, he trusts me, and I think he's motivated to have a go at something challenging. Let's not abandon a book yet again. And besides, this is about his *understanding of the poem—I'll gain some insight into his thinking.*

What do I know about myself as a reader?

I know I'd definitely need to reread the poem several times and I'd jot my thinking in the margins. And I know that if I'm rushed I don't do my best work.

What do I know about teaching kids to read?

Right now it's clear he needs some support from me in order to be successful. He can read the words, so focusing in on comprehension—in this case the strategy of synthesizing—makes sense. Making his thinking visible—through writing—might be a good option. Having to write a little something may help him focus and give him something concrete to do. I'll help him set it up, stay with him as he writes in the first column, and then get out of his way.

Just imagine if I'd said to Emelio at the end of our conference: "Okay, let's get going. You've got five minutes to get something down. Come on, now—let's see how fast you can get this finished." If I'd really said that, I doubt if he'd have ever gotten to "the bird kind of says I need to explore the world because there is more to see." He might *still* be thinking "Your World" is about farmland. Or maybe angels. And even more important, he might never have known that kind of thinking was within him. And nor would I.

☑ Something to Try

If conferring isn't something you regularly do, are you willing to have a go? It might feel awkward or uncomfortable in the beginning, but if you commit to one or two conferences a day for two or three weeks, I'm pretty certain it will become part of your daily routine. Think of it as having a conversation with someone you know and like. Relax. Be yourself. Listen. Don't come armed with a bunch of questions. Begin with something like, "Hey, Jamie, how's your reading going today?" If Jamie says something like, "Good," you might say, "So what's good about it? Tell me more!"

You also might want to do a little research. Divide a page in your notebook in half. On one side, write, "What do I know about Jamie as a reader?" and on the other side write, "What do I know about Jamie now?" Jot some notes in the first column before you confer with Jamie, and do the same after the conference. What do you know about her now that you didn't know before? Would you have learned this in any other way?

Keeping Track of Conferences

I use small, four-by-six-inch spiraled notebooks to help me remember what I learn about kids when I confer with them and what I've taught them. Each child has one, and I write their name with a black Sharpie on the cover. On the back of the front cover, I also include (if I have it) any testing information—areas of strength and areas of concern—to guide me when needed.

I've tried keeping the notebooks at children's tables, but every now and again one would turn up missing, so I kept them in a rectangular plastic basket on my desk. After a conference, I put the notebook back in the basket, upside down and at the back of the row. That way I know with whom I've conferred and with whom I haven't. And because they're at my desk, they're always handy.

FIGURE 8.3
Notes from my conference with Emelio. I also saved a copy of his three-column notes for reference.

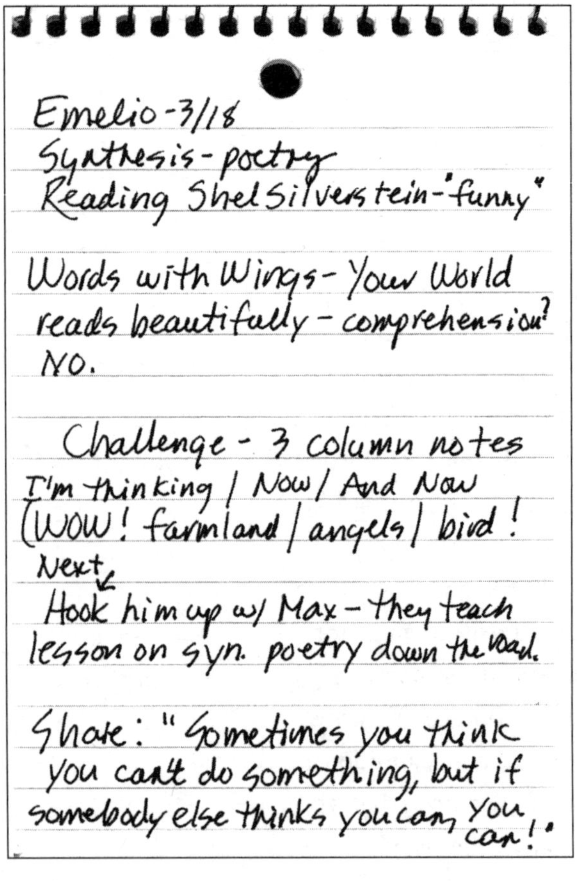
Emelio - 3/18
Synthesis - poetry
Reading Shel Silverstein - "funny"

Words with Wings - Your World
reads beautifully - comprehension?
NO.

Challenge - 3 column notes
I'm thinking / Now / And Now
(WOW! farmland / angels / bird!
Next
Hook him up w/ Max - they teach
lesson on syn. poetry down the road.

Share: "Sometimes you think
you can't do something, but if
somebody else thinks you can, you
can!"

What do I write in them? Sometimes teachers think I'm writing some kind of elaborate, thoughtful essay, but what I'm really doing is jotting down some of what the child says, what I notice the child doing well, where he might need more support, and what I've taught him. Take a look at Emelio's notebook entry in Figure 8.3—you'll get a feel for the kinds of things I record.

It's how we use the notebooks afterward that counts. Once I've conferred with everyone—maybe after six or seven days or so—I close my classroom doors after the kids have gone, get the basket of notebooks, open them to the latest entry, and spread them out—usually on the floor of the meeting area. It's as if the kids are right there with me, only it's oh, so very quiet!

These notebooks, along with children's work samples, my observations, and my own notebook entries help me assess my teaching and my children's learning—they inform and guide my teaching in a big way. When I spread everything out and take a closer look, I consider the implications for whole-class focus lessons, bringing together small groups of children with similar needs for more explicit teaching, creating teaching and learning partnerships, and working with individual children in a variety of ways, based on what I've learned they need. Individually and collectively, I think about where we've been, where we are now, and along with other anecdotal notes and work samples, where it makes the most sense to take children next.

Let's say I have the notebooks spread out and I notice there are four children who need more support when it comes to book selection. I gather their notebooks together with a rubber band, write *book selection* on a small sticky note, and place it on the top of the stack. Or, maybe I notice that three children need more support when it comes to decoding. These three can *say* what to do when they come to a word they don't know, but they don't actually *do* it. Same thing: I bind their notebooks together with a rubber band, write *decoding* on a sticky note, and put it on top of the stack.

When I bring children together in these ways, I'm basing my small-group work on my firsthand knowledge of what children need. In both instances—book selection and decoding—children are not at the same reading level. No matter; their *needs* are the same. I bring children together for small-group work out of efficiency. Reading levels are a consideration, but I don't group children based on level alone.

You might be wondering, "How does guided reading fit into all of this?" I'm with Regie Routman on this one. In *Reading Essentials*, she views guided reading as "any learning context in which the teacher guides one or more students through some aspect of the reading process: choosing books, making sense of text, decoding and defining words, reading fluently, monitoring one's comprehension, determining the author's purpose, and so on" (2003, 151).

So when I look at Dylan's sticky note and write back, "When did John Steptoe use this phrase? What was happening? Why might it be important?" I'm guiding him as a reader. Or when I confer with Emelio about the poem "Your World" and suggest the three-column notes as a way to enhance his understanding, that's guiding him as a reader, too. Even asking children to sit eye-to-eye and knee-to-knee to talk about what they believe is important in the story so far is guiding them as readers.

Connecting Conferences to the Share

When I confer with a child, I notice and name what he is doing well. I also teach him something he needs to know to become a better reader and support him (as needed) in his effort to learn something new. Asking children to articulate this new learning, both for themselves (in the conference) and others (during the share) cements the learning for the reader and gives students opportunities to teach each other.

When I shift the focus of the share from children's reading to themselves as readers, when I ask children questions like the following ones, I've raised the bar significantly:

"What did you learn about yourself as a reader today?"
"What did you learn about yourself today that you didn't know before?"
"What did you learn today that you can use in the days or weeks to come?"
"What did you learn about yourself as a synthesizer of poetry today?"

Now I'm asking kids to reflect, share their thinking, and teach others what they've learned. I invite children I've conferred with to share first—I already know they have something to teach others. Sometimes, too, I'll ask children to get a piece of paper or their notebook, and "show, in pictures and/or words, how you're making sense of our work together today." For examples of this kind of reflection, see Katie's response to the mental files lesson I did with her fourth-grade class (Figure 8.4a, b), and Dylan's response to a class demonstration and discussion on the fine art of conversation (Figure 8.5).

In the beginning, most kids will have no idea what to say when we ask them questions about themselves as readers. And when you think about it, if no one has ever asked them questions like this before, how would they? So now we get to teach them what we mean and explain why learning about ourselves as readers is important. I teach by modeling, of course, but it's during conferences with children that we can be most effective.

I see it this way. We spend important time planning lessons that take children where they need to go next. We give children time to read and

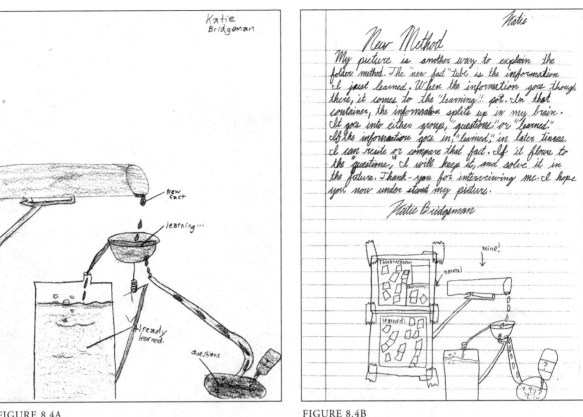

FIGURE 8.4A
Katie's response to the questions, How would you share your understanding of how the mental files lesson works for you? What's your interpretation?

FIGURE 8.4B
When I asked Katie to explain her "learning pot" theory in more detail, she wrote this "New Method" explanation.

practice what we've worked hard to teach them. And then what? We go on to PE or lunch or home without coming back together to debrief what just happened? We just let it go?

We need to harness all that learning and bring it back for everyone! It's part of being a community of learners where we collectively share and teach each other. The expectation is that we *will* learn something today—let's get together to talk about and celebrate it! Every time we confer with children we have the opportunity to teach them something new.

And get this. Remember Emelio? When we all came back together for reflection and sharing, he shared his understanding of "Your World" and the process he used to get there. When asked by an observing teacher if he'd learned anything else about himself as a reader that day, he said, "Well, sometimes you think you can't do something, but if somebody else thinks you can, you can!"

Conversation
On-going
Not working alone
Very expressional
Explaining
Running deeper than the surface
Seeking understanding
An understanding
Try to infer
Infer deeper and deeper
On the moral/lesson
Not too powerful in violence

Dylan

And Remember . . .

■ ■ ■ ■ ■ ■ ■ Do you remember Charles's note at the beginning of Chapter 4—the one that began "Miss Miller," and ended "Love, Charles"? The children and I spent the last hour of my last day in that classroom writing notes and letters to each other. Charles's note was one of the shortest—only thirteen words long—but it's the one that reminds me why I do what I do.

Several years ago now Charles and I happened to run into each other at Dairy Queen. He was with his mom, and the three of us were standing in line to get something cool to drink on a hot summer day. I think I was more excited to see him than he was to see me, but even so I gave him a hug and asked him what he'd been up to since we'd seen each other last. A third grader now, he talked about sports, school, and even what he'd been reading.

"So what have you been up to, Mrs. Miller?" he asked.

"I'm still teaching," I told him, "but I'm working with kids in other teachers' classrooms now."

"Do you like it?"

"I do," I said, "but it's challenging. When I go into classrooms, I don't really know the kids I'm working with. And I'm not usually in the same room for more than a day or two, so it's different. But I'm learning a lot, and that's always good, right?"

At that point I realized this was probably too much information for a nine-year-old, so I ended our chance encounter with a sweet good-bye and a request for his address. I have hundreds of classroom pictures stuffed in that yellow cabinet in my basement, and I decided then and there that it was time to start sending them off.

I sent Charles his, and three or so weeks later I received the following letter from him. If I were to give it a title, I'd call it "Coming Full Circle"!

Dear mrs. miller,
I'm haveing a grate summer.
Thanks for the wonderful pictures.
And gues what? I won state in
swimming 50 free. And I'm
reading about Singgan The Asian
Elephant!
And rememBer When you
walk in to the class room
you are a brilliant
Techer, okay?

Love,

charles

Commentary

Peter Johnston

■ ■ ■ ■ ■ ■

Debbie Miller opens a chapter in this book by observing, "I believe we cannot underestimate the power of our influence—what we choose to say and do in the classroom profoundly affects the ways children view their teacher, themselves, and each other." I fully subscribe to this view. In particular, I believe that the language we use in the classroom affects children's learning in fundamental ways. It affects the ways they interact with and value each other and their diversity, the kinds of literacies they develop, and who they become as literate individuals. The meaning children make of their classroom experiences is mediated by their teacher's language. But more than that, the children are apprenticed into the teacher's ways of talking and interacting, and their interactions with each other are profoundly affected. The effect is magnified the more they aspire to be like the teacher. This understanding might be daunting or even depressing without the rest of the book, in which Debbie shows us how to make the prospect exciting and fulfilling, indeed, the very reason for teaching.

Normally when writing a commentary to a book, we refer to the author by his or her surname—"Miller tells us that . . ."—in order to appear legitimate and academic. In this case, however, it would be incongruous to do so. Reading Debbie Miller's books is like having a chat with a friend and mentor who understands us, has been there, and has useful suggestions when we want them and thoughtful questions to help us think for ourselves. Raising important questions, she answers them *for her* with *her* logic, inviting us to consider them as possibilities, never forcing them on us. Watching Debbie teach is similar to listening in on an ongoing conversation—a comfortable chat with children about literate predilections and practices. It is a comfortableness that belies the power of the teaching. In keeping with the book, then, I will refer to her as "Debbie," without diminishing the intellectual and practical value of her contribution with this book.

The Debbie Miller Factor

Debbie is a remarkable teacher, both of children and of other teachers. I first encountered her some years ago through her videos. I was immediately struck by her ability to be absolutely present for her students. They clearly knew that they had her undivided attention. They mattered to her, unconditionally, and they were engaged in the same project, becoming more fully literate and more fully human through learning together. This presence has been described by Rodgers and Raider-Roth (2006) as "a state of alert awareness, receptivity, and connectedness to the mental, emotional, and physical workings of both the individual and the group in the context of their learning environments, and the ability to respond with a considered and compassionate best next step" (265). It is seen as a sign of a gifted teacher. But, in this book Debbie points out that, as with everything else, "I had to learn how to become reflective on my feet, in the moment." In action, she looks so natural at this it is easy to forget that she *learned* how to become this sort of teacher. In this book she shows us how to develop presence.

In those videos, I was also struck by her ability to articulate the logic of her teaching in engaging and accessible language. Then I read her book *Reading with Meaning* (2002), which expanded the logic and the practical details of her teaching in an even more compelling way. The videos made me want to be like her. The book gave my student teachers and me the tools to do it. My student teachers liked the book for all these reasons—the comfortable writing style, its sheer practicality, and its meaningful orientation. I liked it for these reasons but also for its theoretical consistency and its alignment with research. Debbie's new book is a substantial advance in the direction that research is taking us but is written with a clarity and specificity that university researchers have not yet been able to muster.

Throughout this book we have Debbie's teaching mind on loan. She teaches us by engaging us in the details of a teaching life from inside her mind, showing the thinking behind her teaching and the consequences of her actions—how to notice and what to notice—the view that makes her language choices possible. Of course, she is only doing what she expects us to do, to put our thinking on display by using language intentionally—at once showing, telling, and inviting.

Threads of Language

I have a particular interest in the ways teachers use language to help students make sense of themselves, literacy, and each other as they engage the school day. It was while finishing a book on these matters, *Choice Words: How Our Language Affects Children's Learning*, that I found myself reading Debbie Miller's earlier book, *Reading with Meaning*, and I was so compelled by her language choices that I used examples from her teaching to illustrate productive practices. *Teaching with Intention* offers even more fruitful examples in which we can hear her teach and marvel at the language she chooses. But fortunately we don't have to just marvel at it. She helps us to see not only how to do it—how to think and talk as she does—but why it is important. Listen to her conversation with Emelio as she invites him to reread a poem that he doesn't yet understand:

> **Emelio:** *So you mean, um, you mean I have to read it two* more *times?*
> **DM:** *Well, you don't HAVE to, but I'm thinking that if you did, you might learn something about yourself as a reader of poetry today. You'll be doing some research here that will be important not only for you, but for the whole class. Are you up for it?*

You might say, as she does, that she is negotiating with Emelio. But what I find interesting is what she is offering in the negotiation. She's offering him a new way of being. He had already identified himself as being interested in poetry. He's a poetry kind of guy. She is offering him a way to be even more that kind of guy. But she's offering more. She offers him the opportunity to become a researcher, too, and in that capacity to contribute to the community's knowledge. Beyond that, she puts it to him as a good-natured challenge, "Are you up for it?" with those as the stakes. If he picks up the challenge and pulls it off, and she will make sure he does, then he builds a stronger sense of agency. And by understanding that he contributes to the community with his efforts, as well as himself, he expands his sense of the community and accepts that it is normal to want to contribute to it.

As you will see in the book, these interactions are not isolated conversational events, but consistent threads in her classroom talk. For example, when she sends the children off to pursue their reading and writing, she comments to them, "I can't wait to see what we find out." "We," she says, our community (again). At the same time, she sends them off expecting to be surprised and expecting them to have their teacher's interest along with that of their fellow community members.

When a student offers an unexpected interpretation of a text, many teachers would respond by trying to correct the student's thinking. Debbie takes a very different stance, saying, "I'm going to have to go back and look more closely at that part again. I was thinking he was going to keep following his dream, but now I'm not so sure. Thanks for getting me thinking, Ramon!" She is not interested in there being a single correct perspective, though she puts hers out there for him to consider. She is much more interested in conveying to the student that his thinking matters, that she is interested in learning from him, and at the same time conveying to the others in the class that multiple perspectives should be expected and that when someone offers a different perspective, it might be a good place to learn. She is less interested in his comprehension than in his comprehending, and his (and his peers') conceptualization of what they are doing individually and collectively.

Beyond Language

But it isn't only through the spoken language that we influence children's literate development. We apprentice them into ways of being literate together through the ways we organize the classroom. Debbie makes her thinking about the spatial, temporal, and organizational design of classrooms available to us as well, along with the consequences for students. In other words, Debbie shows us how, through our uses of language, time, and space, we can structure the warp on which, in collaboration with our students, we can weave the most valued designs of classroom life. She encourages us to teach with intention—to decide what we want, to have a vision of literacy before we start, and then to plan and act so that we will achieve our intention.

To help us with this, she first reminds us of what we might intend, showing us what the bigger goals of education can be. She expands our imagination of what is possible by example. For instance, she describes the beliefs of children in her anchor classes in the following terms:

They see themselves and each other as kids with purpose; they see themselves as the kind of kids who can figure things out. These children

> *sense that they have the capacity to roll up their sleeves, take action, and get things done.*

This is what I refer to as a sense of agency (Johnston 2004). I believe this is the foundation of a disposition toward resilience. She also describes the ways children learn to engage with each other. For example, she notes that children in these classes

> *talk and look at* each other; *responses are not directed to the teacher unless she joins in with a question or comment. And no one feels the need to raise their hand. And what's the teacher doing during all of this? She's off to the side, listening carefully, taking notes. The kids are very much in charge.*

She also shows us why this vision is important, why children must be in charge of their own literate learning and thinking—only then do they actually know how to structure their literate lives in the future without others doing it for them. From my perspective, these interactions suggest that the children are developing a sense of reciprocity, the sense that through interacting together as equals, with differences, they can expand their own understanding. They become, in fact, in control of their own development.

Consistent with this vision, Debbie does not address classroom management as a separate matter. There is, of course, no question that classroom management is crucial to effective literacy instruction, and Debbie provides the necessary management details. However, she offers us two important advances on this. First, she shows us the reciprocal relationship between management and effective instruction. Second, she shows us that if we want children to learn to manage themselves, they have to be involved in designing the tools for self-management. Showing the wisdom of Marie Clay's (1991) injunction to put children in control of their reading, writing, and learning processes, she ensures that from the start children are fully engaged in organizing the classroom, managing their learning, and anticipating their own learning needs. As she puts it, by doing so they'll "learn a thing or two about thoughtful organization, *and*, because they've been part of the placement process, they'll know firsthand where things are kept, why it makes sense to keep them there, and where to put things back . . . the why, the what for, and the how to."

Systematically building individual and collaborative independence is one of the hallmarks of Debbie's teaching.

How easy it is for the pressures of testing and school life to distract us from these goals. And these are not the kinds of teaching goals that show up on state standards or in basal teacher's guides, but if we lose sight of them, then we are teaching for different, and I would argue diminished, purposes. We will make different decisions about our teaching practices. In showing us these children, Debbie expands our vision of what is possible for children's literacy education, what we can aim for; then she shows us how to intentionally teach to achieve that vision. She also offers observations that might be useful for politicians and administrators who are inclined to lean on the coercive pressures of testing to hurry teaching along. For example, she notes, "I can't be looking at the clock every few minutes thinking about what's next. I have to be actively engaged in what's happening now, at this precise moment." In other words, if we want teachers like Debbie, high-stakes testing might not be the way to accomplish that goal since it reduces the possibility of teachers being present for their children.

Genius and the Magic of Teaching

It is tempting to think about Debbie as simply a gifted teacher—to be admired like a work of art produced by genius. But she is very quick to draw a moustache on this image for us, as she does with her students. She talks about her teaching historically with all the blemishes and discoveries, so we get to see that this isn't just genius at work. We see *how* she came to be the teacher we aspire to be like. Through her own experiences and those of other teachers, she shows us how children and teachers, including herself, got to where they are now. She reveals, "I used to think . . ." and, "I know, because I remember a time when I . . ." and that earlier in her teaching, "So intently was I listening *for* thinking that mirrored my own that I'd forgotten the importance of listening *to* what kids have to say." Centrally, Debbie asks and answers the question: "How did I go from managing a classroom to creating a classroom community responsive to student needs and interests, a classroom focused less on activities and more on thinking and understanding?"

In a way, she takes the magic out of teaching by slowing it down and showing the process. And yet, having read the book, I am reminded of how magical teaching is. The magic she keeps is the joyfulness, the accomplishment, and the inspiration—the big stuff of teaching. The magic she takes away is the myth of genius. She shows us the work, the learning, the inevitable trials and errors that get us to a place that is never an end, but another place to learn.

References

Clay, Marie. 1991. *Becoming Literate: The Construction of Inner Control.* Portsmouth, NH: Heinemann.

Johnston, Peter H. 2004. *Choice Words: How Our Language Affects Children's Learning.* Portland, ME: Stenhouse.

Rodgers, Carol R., and Miriam B. Raider-Roth. 2006. "Presence in Teaching." *Teachers and Teaching* 12 (3): 265–287.

Lesson Design Tool

Lesson Design

What is the focus of the lesson? What do I want students to learn?

Why is this important? How will it help students?

How do I use this skill or strategy myself?

What connections can I help students make?

Reflections

What did I learn from my students during the workshop?

Next Steps

Where do I/we need to go next with our learning?

Showing Students How

Modeling/Thinking Aloud

■ What books and/or materials will I need?

Demonstration

■ Are there structures or formats that I need to show students how to do?

Guided Practice

■ How will I release responsibility to students during the lesson?

■ Will students and I co-construct an anchor chart? What is its focus?

Guided and Independent Practice

What books and/or materials will students need?

_____
_____
_____
_____

What do I want students to do:

■ individually _____

■ and/or in pairs _____

■ and/or in small groups _____

What will I do?

_____ confer   _____ observe
_____ listen in   _____ meet with students in small groups

Reflect, Share, Teach

Guiding questions for students

■ What did you learn (content)? How will you teach us?

■ What did you learn about yourself as a reader today that you didn't know before (process)? How will you teach us?

Children's Literature

Berger, Melvin and Gilda. 2000. *What Do Sharks Eat for Dinner? Questions and Answers About Sharks.* New York: Scholastic.

Bruchac, Joseph. 1992. *Thirteen Moons on Turtle's Back: A Native American Year of Moons.* New York: Philomel.

Cole, Joanna. 1986. *Hungry, Hungry Sharks!* New York: Scholastic.

Dubowski, Cathy. 1998. *Shark Attack!* New York: DK.

Edwards, Pamela Duncan. 1998. *Barefoot: Escape on the Underground Railroad.* New York: HarperTrophy.

Gilpin, Daniel. 2005. *Life-Size Sharks and Other Underwater Creatures.* New York: Sterling.

Hopkinson, Deborah. 1995. *Sweet Clara and the Freedom Quilt.* New York: Dragonfly Books.

Janeczko, Paul, ed. 1990. *The Place My Words Are Looking For: What Poets Say About and Through Their Work.* New York: Bradbury.

Johnson, Georgia Douglas. 2000. "Your World." In *Words with Wings: A Treasury of African-American Poetry and Art.* Ed. Belinda Rochelle. New York: HarperCollins.

Johnston, Tony. 2004. *The Harmonica.* Watertown, MA: Charlesbridge.

Llewellyn, Claire. 1999. *My Best Book of Sharks.* Boston: Kingfisher.

Macquitty, Miranda. 2004. *Shark.* New York: DK.

Mark, Jan. 1999. *The Midas Touch.* Cambridge, MA: Candlewick.

Mugford, Simon. 2005. *Sharks and Other Dangers of the Deep.* New York: St. Martin's.

Muth, John. 2002. *The Three Questions: Based on a Story by Leo Tolstoy.* New York: Scholastic.

Nelson, Kristin. 2003. *Hunting Sharks.* Minneapolis, MN: Lerner.

Parker, Steve. 2006. *100 Things You Should Know About Sharks.* Great Bardfield, UK: Miles Kelly.

Rappaport, Doreen. 2000. *Freedom River.* New York: Hyperion.

Rochelle, Belinda, ed. 2000. *Words with Wings: A Treasury of African-American Poetry and Art.* New York: HarperCollins.

Rylant, Cynthia. 2006. *The Journey: Stories of Migration.* New York: Blue Sky Press.

Savage, Stephen. 2005. *See-Through Sharks.* Philadelphia: Running Press.

Say, Allen. 2000. *The Sign Painter.* New York: Houghton Mifflin.

Serio, John, ed. 2005. *Poetry for Young People: The Seasons.* New York: Sterling.

Silverstein, Shel. 1974. *Where the Sidewalk Ends.* New York: Harper and Row.

Simon, Seymour. 2005. *Sharks.* New York: Scholastic.

Steptoe, John. 1984. *The Story of Jumping Mouse.* New York: Lothrop, Lee & Shepard.

TIME for Kids and Adrienne Betz. 2005. *Sharks!* New York: HarperTrophy.

Winter, Jeanette. 2005. *The Librarian of Basra: A True Story from Iraq.* Orlando, FL: Harcourt.

———. 1988. *Follow the Drinking Gourd.* New York: Knopf.

Wright, Courtni Crump. 1994. *Journey to Freedom: A Story of the Underground Railroad.* New York: Holiday House.

References

Allington, Richard. 2005. *What Really Matters for Struggling Readers: Designing Research-Based Programs.* 2nd ed. New York: Allyn & Bacon.

Bombeck, Erma. 1971. *If Life Is a Bowl of Cherries, What Am I Doing in the Pits?* New York: Fawcett.

Calkins, Lucy. 1983. *Lessons from a Child.* Portsmouth, NH: Heinemann.

Clay, Marie. 1998. *By Different Paths to Common Outcomes.* Portland, ME: Stenhouse.

Garrison, Catherine, and Michael Erlinghaus. "Formative and Summative Assessments in the Classroom." National Middle School Association. http://www.nmsa.org/Publications/ WebExclusive/Assessment/tabid/1120/Default.aspx.

Hansen, Jane. 1987. *When Writers Read.* Portsmouth, NH: Heinemann.

Harvey, Stephanie, and Anne Goudvis. 2007. *Strategies That Work: Teaching Comprehension for Understanding and Engagement.* 2nd ed. Portland, ME: Stenhouse.

Harwayne, Shelley. 2000. *Lifetime Guarantees: Toward Ambitious Literacy Teaching.* Portsmouth, NH: Heinemann.

Johnston, Peter. 2004. *Choice Words: How Our Language Affects Children's Learning.* Portland, ME: Stenhouse.

Keene, Ellin Oliver. 2008. *To Understand: New Horizons in Reading Comprehension.* Portsmouth, NH: Heinemann.

Miller, Debbie. 2002. *Reading with Meaning: Teaching Comprehension in the Primary Grades.* Portland, ME: Stenhouse.

Pearson, P. David, and Margaret C. Gallagher. 1983. "The Instruction of Reading Comprehension." *Contemporary Educational Psychology* 8 (3): 317–344.

Pearson, P. David, Laura R. Roehler, Janice A. Dole, and Gerard G. Duffy. 1992. "Developing Expertise in Reading Comprehension." In *What Research Has to Say About Reading Instruction.* Ed. Alan E. Farstrup and S. Jay Samuels. Newark, DE: International Reading Association.

Perkins, David. 2003. "Making Thinking Visible." New Horizons for Learning. http://www.newhorizons.org/strategies/thinking/ perkins.htm.

Peterson, Ralph. 1992. *Life in a Crowded Place: Making a Learning Community.* Portsmouth, NH: Heinemann.

Piaget, Jean. 1983. "Piaget's Theory." In *Handbook of Child Psychology.* Ed. P. Mussen. New York: Wiley.

Ritchhart, Ron. 2002. *Intellectual Character: What It Is, Why It Matters, and How to Get It.* San Francisco: Jossey-Bass.

Routman, Regie. 2003. *Reading Essentials: The Specifics You Need to Teach Reading Well.* Portsmouth, NH: Heinemann.

Smith, Frank. 1998. *The Book of Learning and Forgetting.* New York: Teachers College Press.

Index